THE GREAT
BARRIER REEF

A JOURNEY THROUGH THE WORLD'S GREATEST NATURAL WONDER

THE GREAT BARRIER REEF

A JOURNEY THROUGH THE WORLD'S GREATEST NATURAL WONDER

LEN ZELL

BBC
EARTH

www.bbcearth.com

MURDOCH BOOKS

www.bbcearth.com

CONTENTS

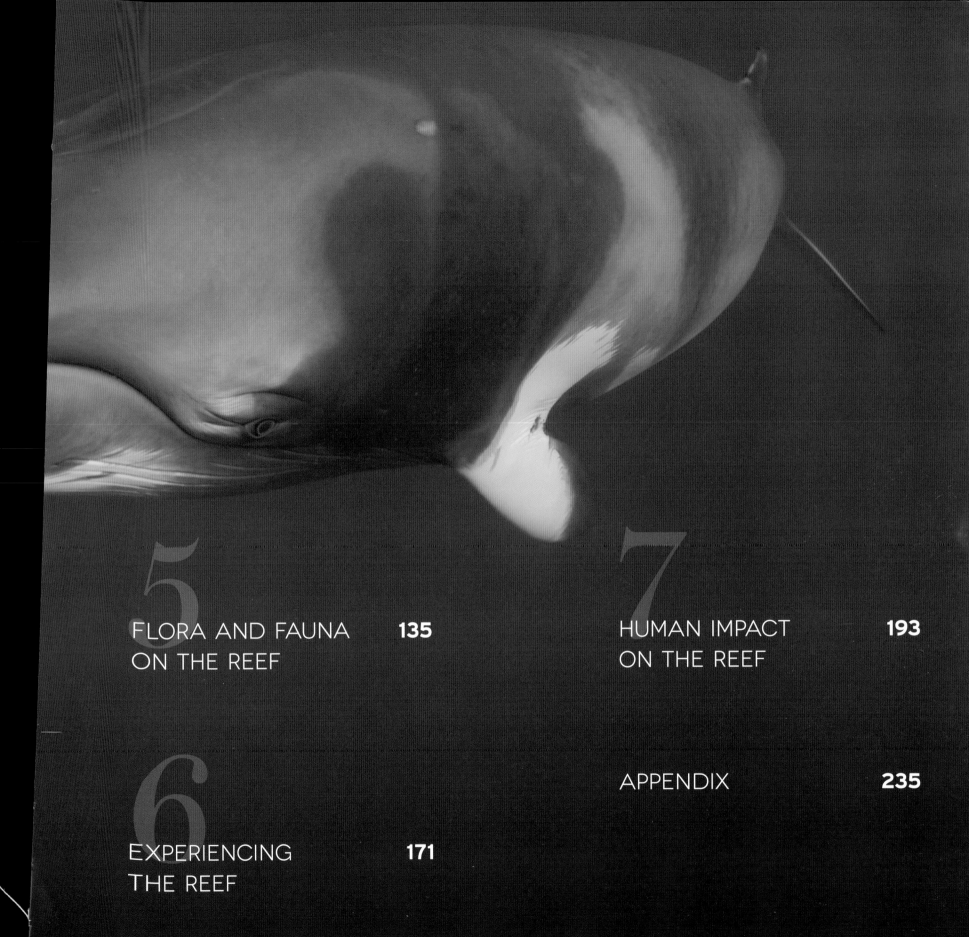

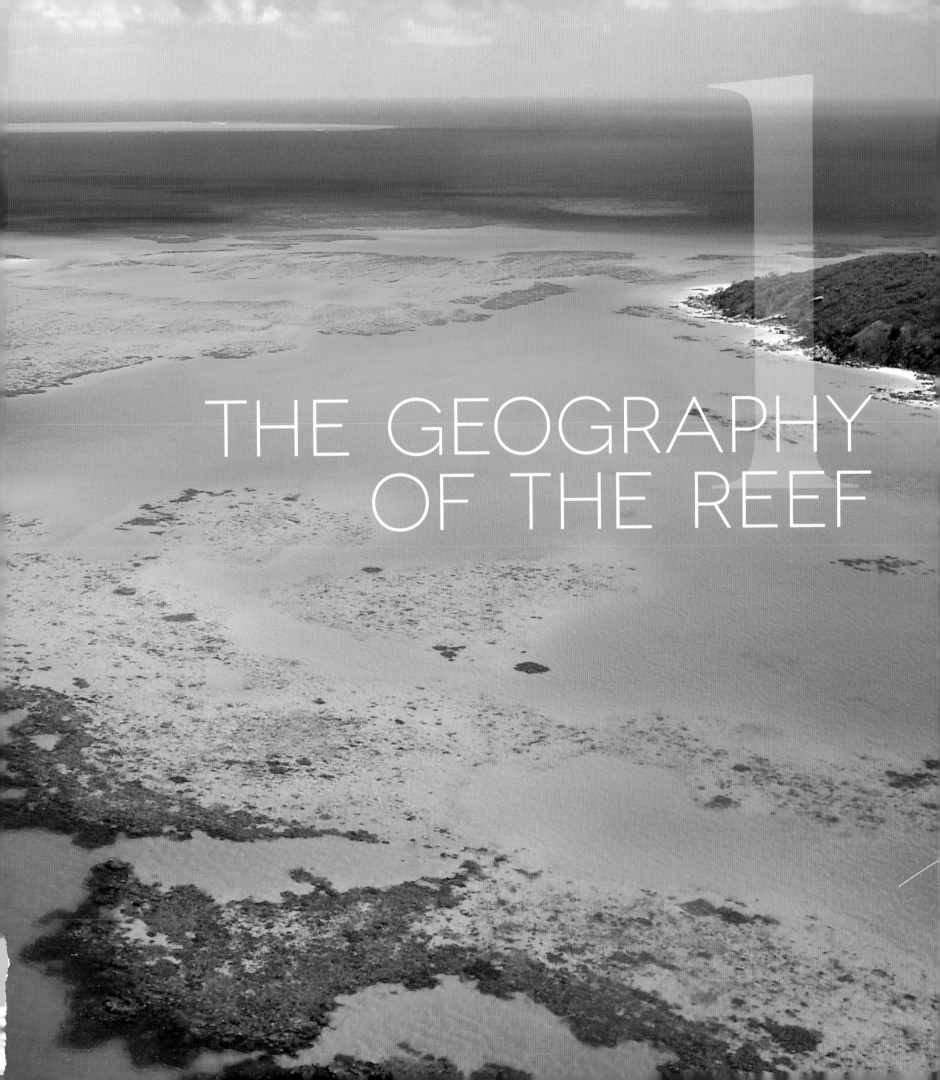

THE GEOGRAPHY
OF THE REEF

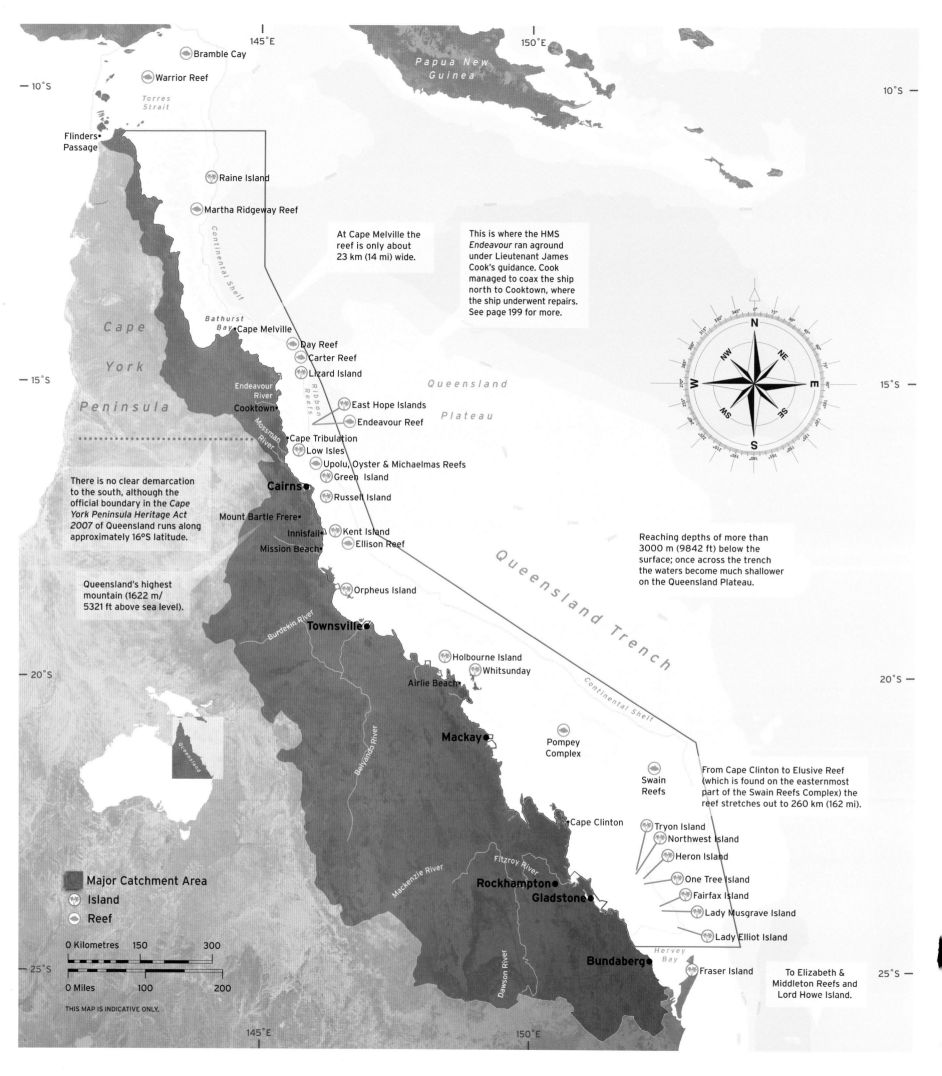

Bramble Cay

Warrior Reef

Torres Strait

— 10°S

145°E

150°E

Papua New Guinea

10°S —

Flinders•
Passage

Raine Island

Martha Ridgeway Reef

Continental Shelf

At Cape Melville the reef is only about 23 km (14 mi) wide.

This is where the HMS *Endeavour* ran aground under Lieutenant James Cook's guidance. Cook managed to coax the ship north to Cooktown, where the ship underwent repairs. See page 199 for more.

Bathurst Bay

•Cape Melville

Day Reef

Carter Reef

Lizard Island

C a p e

Queensland

Y o r k

— 15°S

Endeavour River

East Hope Islands

Endeavour Reef

P e n i n s u l a

Cooktown•

Plateau

15°S —

Ribbon Reefs

Mossman River

•Cape Tribulation

Low Isles

Upolu, Oyster & Michaelmas Reefs

CAIRNS•

Green Island

There is no clear demarcation to the south, although the official boundary in the *Cape York Peninsula Heritage Act 2007* of Queensland runs along approximately 16°S latitude.

Russell Island

Mount Bartle Frere•

Innisfail•

Kent Island

Ellison Reef

Mission Beach•

Reaching depths of more than 3000 m (9842 ft) below the surface; once across the trench the waters become much shallower on the Queensland Plateau.

Queensland's highest mountain (1622 m/ 5321 ft above sea level).

Orpheus Island

Burdekin River

Q u e e n s l a n d   T r e n c h

Townsville•

— 20°S

Holbourne Island

Whitsunday

20°S —

Airlie Beach•

Continental Shelf

Queensland

Belyando River

Mackay•

Pompey Complex

From Cape Clinton to Elusive Reef (which is found on the easternmost part of the Swain Reefs Complex) the reef stretches out to 260 km (162 mi).

Swain Reefs

Mackenzie River

Fitzroy River

•Cape Clinton

Tryon Island

Northwest Island

Heron Island

Major Catchment Area

Island

Reef

Rockhampton•

One Tree Island

Fairfax Island

Gladstone•

Lady Musgrave Island

0 Kilometres 150   300

Lady Elliot Island

Dawson River

Hervey Bay

— 25°S

0 Miles   100   200

Bundaberg•

•Fraser Island

25°S —

To Elizabeth & Middleton Reefs and Lord Howe Island.

THIS MAP IS INDICATIVE ONLY.

145°E

150°E

What is the Great Barrier Reef?

Internationally recognised as the greatest reef system on Earth, the Great Barrier Reef conjures up images of azure waters teeming with colourful fish against a background of corals and algae of every shape, form and colour. This amazing system, which runs along the northeastern coast of the Australian continent, almost to Papua New Guinea, represents about 10 per cent of the coral reefs in the world. Easily accessed via many coastal jump-off points, the Reef is a unique location, and one of the world's most popular tourism destinations.

In this book you will meet many of the Reef's fascinating plants and animals, which interact in bizarre communities seldom seen by humans, and also learn about their habitats and island and reef communities. And if you plan to visit the Reef some time in the future, you will discover how to make the most of your visit.

The Great Barrier Reef is part of the Indo-Pacific coral reefs, which extend from Africa and Madagascar eastwards to Easter Island, a territory of Chile, in the Pacific Ocean. In the midst of the Indo-Pacific coral reefs lies the 'hotspot' of reef diversity in the Coral Triangle, bounded by eastern Indonesia, the Philippines and Solomon Islands. Here the greatest number of all coral reef species in the world can be found.

The Great Barrier Reef extends from Bramble Cay in the north to Lady Elliot Island in the south—more than 2300 km (1429 mi)—but

attractive coral reef systems continue down the east coast of Australia to Lord Howe Island, the southernmost coral reef in the Pacific. In the north, the reef systems extend east and west into the Coral and Arafura seas, respectively, joining up with the Coral Triangle around Papua New Guinea.

To the east of the Reef, past the 3000-m (9842-ft) deep Queensland Trench, is a series of isolated coral reefs—known as the Coral Sea Reefs—on the Queensland Rise in the north and the Lord Howe Rise (Lord Howe Island and Elizabeth and Middleton reefs) in the south. Under Australian jurisdiction, they are known as the Coral Sea Territories. At Cape Melville, the Reef is only about 23 km (14 mi) wide, but in the south, it stretches out to 260 km (162 mi) wide, from Cape Clinton to Elusive Reef, which is the easternmost part of the Swain Reefs complex.

In the Reef are more than 3000 individual reefs and almost 1300 islands, including the 400 islands in Torres Strait, making it one of the single largest ecosystems on the planet. Each reef is constructed of pure limestone produced by animals and algae—except those reefs near land, which may include some sediment.

Shelf-edge reefs have a flat top, formed by the tide, with a 'front' that faces the prevailing waves. Each front has a steep slope down into the abyssal depths of the edge of the continental shelf, the area of shallow seas around the perimeter of the conti-nent. On the backs of the reefs, the slopes drop to

Previous spread: A coral reef, part of Lizard Island National Park. Once the sea level rose thousands of years ago, this higher ground was cut off from the mainland, forming an island, which was named by Lieutenant James Cook for all the goannas found there.

Opposite: The Great Barrier Reef region map, showing the main islands and reefs.

3

the continental shelf, which is, on average, about 40 m (131 ft) deep as far as the coast.

Coral reefs could be called algal/coral reefs because of the very important roles played by a variety of algae. Some are hard coralline forms called 'paint algae', as they look like a thick coat of paint. They form ramparts on the fronts of reefs and also cement old and broken coral colonies together to form the matrix you see as a coral reef. Meanwhile, wave action, currents, low tide exposure, cyclonic storms and coral- and algae-eating animals can all help demolish these coral structures, which eventually form sand or rubble deposits; these in turn can accumulate into coral cays (see page 10).

Above: A thriving ecosystem on a back reef. This slope on the lee side of a coral reef may lead into a lagoon on the open sea.

Defining the Great Barrier Reef

The Great Barrier Reef sits on the continental shelf of Queensland and Torres Strait. There are several ways to define it, but the major source of information on this unique system is the Great Barrier Reef Marine Park Authority (known as GBRMPA, or 'gabroompa'), although its statistics are incomplete. Here's the background.

In 1968 W.G.H. Maxwell, a geologist, provided the first definition of the 'Great Barrier Reef Province'. There are three regions: the Northern Region—all the reefs to the south of Bramble Cay in Torres Strait, which are characterised by shallow waters (less than 40 m/131 ft deep); the Central Region—from Mackay to Innisfail along the mainland coast (down to 40-60 m/131-197 ft deep); and the Southern Region—from the southern boundary of the Central Region south to Lady Elliot Island (with depths to 160 m/525 ft). Maxwell also used the 200 m (656 ft) depth contour as the eastern edge and the coastline as the western boundary.

Most researchers used Maxwell's description until the formation in 1975 of the Great Barrier Reef Marine Park Authority, which was established to manage the Great Barrier Reef Marine Park—at 345,000 square km (133,205 square mi), the largest marine park in the world. The Queensland government insisted on leaving out 'Queensland waters', which included all areas from the high tide mark on islands and the mainland down to the low water mark, and some areas for 'future port or similar developments' along the coast, out to 5 nautical miles off the coast. In 1981 the Great Barrier Reef Region was declared a World Heritage Area or WHA (348,000 square km or 134,000 square mi), which includes not only the entire Marine Park Region but also the Queensland waters and islands (about 2 per cent of the WHA) previously excluded from the Region. This action prevented any mining or oil drilling from being carried out in the GBRWHA.

The Queensland government later adopted mirror Marine Park legislation. Neither the GBRMPA nor the GBRWHA include Torres Strait north of latitude 10°41'S. This is now an area of cooperative management with Papua New Guinea.

While the box on page 5 gives you some idea of the immensity of the Great Barrier Reef system and the areas with which it interacts, it is important to realise that coral species come and go. At present it seems that the diversity of coral and fish species on the Great Barrier Reef is decreasing, possibly as a result of climate change, overfishing, and contamination by chemicals and sediments transported by rivers from agriculture, mining and urbanisation in Queensland and Papua New Guinean watersheds. The species loss may be as high as 40–60 per cent in some areas of the Reef.

The Reef, as defined by Maxwell, has about 325 species of coral in the north, 280 in Torres Strait, 343 in the Central Section and 244 in the Capricorn and Bunker Group on the inner shelf in the south.

Understanding reefs

The first time you dip your head underwater on the Reef, you'll probably feel overwhelmed by the range of colours, shapes, movements and sounds. Allow yourself plenty of time. Start by focusing on one or two animals, then gradually take in more and more—all the variations in form, activity and relationships.

Queensland's continental shelf is the base for both the present-day Great Barrier Reef and the many older layers of previous fossil 'Great Barrier Reefs', from those periods when the reefs were dry during glaciations.

Different reef shapes reveal varying historical geology, climate, weather, oceanic currents and tidal forces. There is also an enormous diversity of habitats on the sea floor between the reefs, leading into mudflat and seagrass communities on the coast, which features rich mangroves, rainforests, estuaries and savannah grasslands.

The Great Barrier Reef has no atolls—those coral islands that form around lagoons—and the greatest reef variations are seen across the shelf rather than from north to south.

On top of some reefs—for example, Warrior Reef in Torres Strait—there are rich mangrove communities that appear to be built on a mud base,

If one part of the Great Barrier Reef is damaged by a natural disaster or human activity, other parts also suffer.

unlike those further south, which are based on the skeletal remains of coral and algae.

Continuing research enhances our understanding of these reefs, the life on and between them, and also their origins. On every surface in every ecosystem associated with the Reef there is a covering of living things, from bacteria to rainforest trees. Usually the larger the organism, the more it has been studied.

Fringing reefs

Fringing reefs run close to the shore, with little or no lagoon between the inner edge of the reef and the land. Some fringing reefs have grown on sand, gravel and other sediments washed out or deposited there during the last low ice age, when the sea level was 130 m (427 ft) lower than it is now. Along the mainland coast these reefs vary from remnants of previous healthy systems to those, in the far north, that remain relatively healthy today.

Almost all mainland islands, which are exposed hills or mountaintops across the continental shelf, are fringed by reefs; however, on the weather side of many islands facing the prevailing southeasterly winds, there may only be a veneer of living corals on their rocky surfaces.

Platform reefs

Many of these shelf-edge reefs, which vary in size from 200 square m to 50,000 ha (239 square yd to 123,553 acres), feature lagoons varying in depth from less than a metre (3 ft) to 30 m (98 ft). These reefs, such as Warrior Reef in Torres Strait, can be found throughout the Great Barrier Reef, right across the continental shelf to the outer edge.

Coral cays

Found on some platform reefs, coral cays can range from small ephemeral sand bars to permanent islands more than 100 ha (247 acres) in area. They are formed from materials eroded off the sides and top of the reef, then accumulated on top of its lee side, where the waves hit and wrap around the reef. There the waves meet front on, dropping loads of sediment. Cays can be formed from almost pure foram sand (comprising minute single-celled animals), coral and shell materials or the rubble from larger coral skeletons.

Ribbon reefs

Ribbon reefs are found primarily between Cairns and Southern Cape York Peninsula. They are long (up to 30 km/18 mi) and narrow (mostly less than 600 m/656 yd), and run north–south along the edge of the continental shelf. Most curve inwards at each end, where the inflowing oceanic waters stimulate coral growth—these are called cuspate ribbon reefs. The floors of the channels between ribbon reefs, probably the remains of a previous reef system more than 40,000 years old, tend to be scoured clean by ocean currents.

Previous spread: Reef edges present a 'wall of mouths', all intent on devouring any food or nutrients that move past them.

Opposite: Staghorn coral on a platform reef off Heron Island, a coral cay near the Tropic of Capricorn in the southern part of the Great Barrier Reef.

Left: Windjana Gorge, Napier Range, Western Australia. These old coral reefs, which were formed about 350 million years ago, are more than 2 km (1 mi) deep. Divers will recognise the fissures and caves cut into these ancient karst limestone surfaces as being similar to the ones they would see underwater on the Great Barrier Reef. See page 137 for more information.

Dissected and deltaic reefs

These reefs, which grow along the edge of the shelf adjacent to Cape York Peninsula, appear to be eroding as fast as they grow. Due to the shallow nature of the shelf here as well as the strong water flows, you can see the development of deltas both inside and outside the channels between the reefs. You can also see deltas formed on the reef channels in the Pompey Complex, where there is a 4-m (13-ft) tidal range with very fast currents in channels that are as deep as 100 m (327 ft).

In several sections of the Reef—for example, off Cairns and the Pompey Complex—there are older submerged reefs running parallel to the eastern sides of the outer reefs; these were caused when the shelf sank under the pressure of encroaching seawater during the last rise in sea level.

Human activity on the Reef

The first humans to experience the Great Barrier Reef were the Aboriginal Australians, who made their way into Australia during one of the periods of low sea levels between the last few glaciations, about 100,000–50,000 years ago. About 42,000 years ago, the sea level fell, reaching 130 m (427 ft) below current levels about 18,000 years ago.

The Aboriginals would have followed the coast out to the edge of the continental shelf and seen the reefs as flat-topped limestone hills or limestone outcrops (see page 195). You can see similar karst landscapes at Windjana Gorge in the Napier Range of Western Australia. This 350-million-year-old reef system is now high and dry. Karst landscapes can also be found in many other parts of the world where volcanic uplift has brought old reefs well above present sea levels.

Many people have dreamed of finding an underwater cave on the Great Barrier Reef that provides evidence not only of the dry period from about 40,000 to 12,000 years ago but also of human usage of the sites. In one such cave at 25 m (82 ft)

Opposite: Soft corals grow on the SS *Yongala* shipwreck (see page 46), a heritage site that is encrusted with life.

Right: A diver investigates the life forms under a ledge. As coral colonies grow together, they can form underwater caves and arches.

Far right: The orange sea fan, a type of soft coral, is made up of thousands of tiny polyps, which form a flexible skeleton with a branch-like appearance.

deep on Tijou Reef, 2-m (6½-ft) cores indicate terrestial sediments from more than 4000 years ago.

As the sea rose at an average of about 1.3 cm (½ in) per year from 18,000 years to 6000 years ago, this would have forced the Aboriginal people across the continental shelf onto the mainland at today's sea level.

Both Aboriginal Australians and Torres Strait Islanders lay claim to 'Sea Country', traditionally used areas on many islands and reefs. There are many sites of archaeological significance on most mainland islands, with burial sites, rock paintings, middens and some cays with evidence of past use. Prior to European settlement, Aboriginal people in the drier catchment areas used a technique called 'firestick farming'—the practice of burning off vegetation when hunting—so this would have had some effect on the Reef over the last 18,000 years.

At least 500 years ago and possibly as far back as 5000 years ago, the Makassar people from Malaya were probably fishing for beche-de-mer (sea cucumbers) in the northern sections of the Great Barrier Reef. They were followed by Portuguese sailors, the first Europeans to travel down the west coast of Cape York (see page 195) in the fifteenth century. Then in 1770 Lieutenant James Cook 'discovered' the Great Barrier Reef when he was two-thirds

along its length to the northeast of Cairns and ran aground on Endeavour Reef. He eventually found a route out of the Reef, between Day and Carter reefs, now called Cook's Passage (see also page 199).

Cook's voyage became the spearhead for further European exploration, resulting in activities such as massive land clearing and agriculture, mining and urban development in the mid-1850s. These all had significant impacts on the Reef—especially on the coastal fringing reefs. Rivers became silted up, the sea floors were modified and the water quality deteriorated. One of the last rivers to suffer a similar fate was the Mossman River, which silted up in the 1920s, soon after the land was cleared for sugar-cane farming. Previously the river had been navigable by mid-sized ships carrying the sugar cane out and delivering supplies.

There are many shipwrecks along the coast and on the Reef, with some thirty classified as historic sites and many still to be found or verified. The construction of lighthouses at key locations gradually defined safe shipping routes through the Reef and, as modern technology has taken over, all the lighthouses have become fully automated, with many of the older ones, such as the Raine Island beacon (see page 203), remaining as national heritage sites of historical importance.

Protecting the Reef

The GBRMPA was formed in 1975, nearly 100 years after the significant deterioration of the Great Barrier Reef had begun. Fishermen who began using the Reef for spearfishing in the 1950s have described how, over time, fish stocks decreased and water quality deteriorated. As these people aged and witnessed the deterioration of the Reef, many became fierce conservationists.

Between 1975 and 2005 the total commercial and recreational fish catch doubled, and coastal runoff from rivers and creeks increased up to ten times (depending on which catchment was being studied). These issues, along with climate change and its associated effects, are a real challenge for the Great Barrier Reef.

Since Matthew Flinders charted its inner route between 1801 and 1803 (see page 202), the Great Barrier Reef has become a very important shipping route. Today you can see many vessels—carrying bauxite, copper, lead, nickel, coal, oil, gas and many other products—moving through the region. When one of these hits a reef and leaks its load into the waters, it causes a major environmental catastrophe.

There is also a significant trawling fleet operating in the region, primarily for prawns (shrimp), and the devastating impact of these ships on the sea floor ecosystem has been well-documented. The Great Barrier Reef Marine Park Authority has now restricted their operations and other extractive industries to smaller areas of the Great Barrier Reef.

Tourism vessels and aircraft operate from many jump-off points along the coast, bringing billions of dollars each year to these areas. Visitors head to resorts on coral cays and mainland islands, pontoons moored on selected reefs or to moorings, while divers and fishers who hold permits roam specially designated areas.

The Great Barrier Reef south of the northern tip of Cape York is protected by the Great Barrier Reef Marine Park (GBRMP), which uses a zoning system (see page 217) in an effort to minimise the impact of human use, such as runoff, climate change, coral bleaching, outbreaks of crown-of-thorns sea star, fishing and tourism. Queensland Marine Parks staff monitor all these activities—it is not uncommon to be pulled up in the middle of nowhere by staff to ensure you are obeying the rules. The Reef, and its creatures, are worth it.

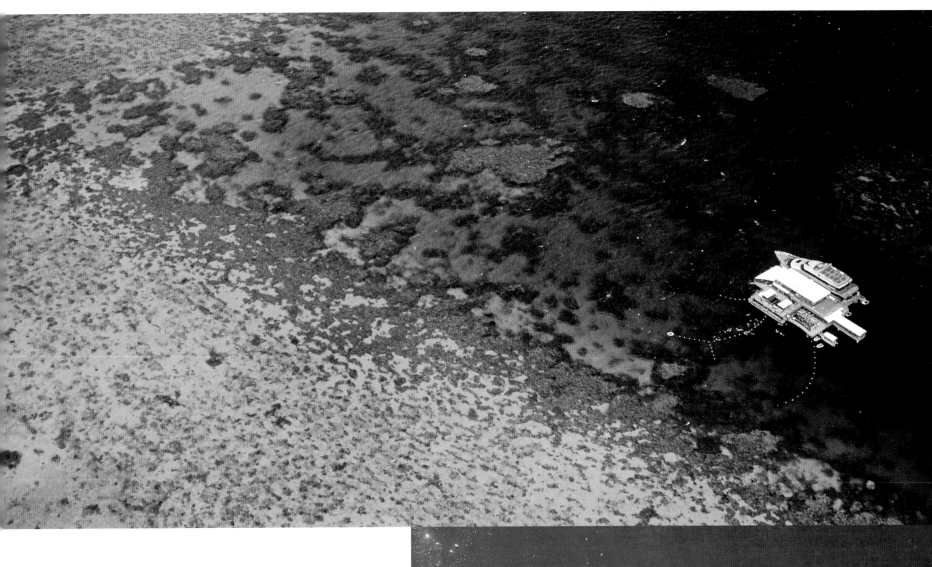

Opposite left: A cargo ship leaks oil onto the Great Barrier Reef, where groundings occur almost every year.

Opposite right: A fishing fleet moored in the Mooloolah River, at Mooloolaba on the Sunshine Coast, Queensland.

Above: Visitors to the Reef can use pontoons such as this as a base for snorkelling, diving and viewing the coral reef in GBRMPA designated areas.

Right: A marine biologist injects copper sulfate into a crown-of-thorns sea star feeding on its preferred prey, *Acropora* plate coral. The copper sulfate is effective at killing the pest but results in heavy metal pollution.

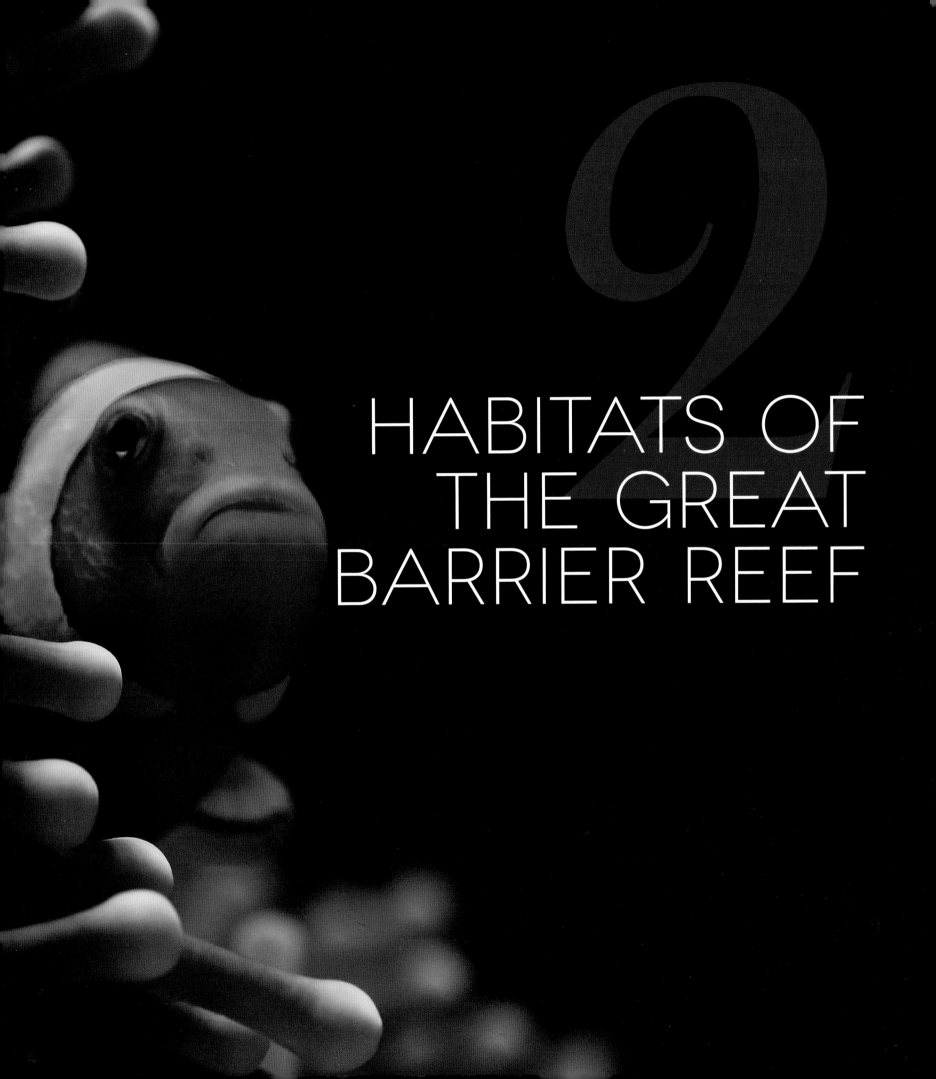

2
HABITATS OF THE GREAT BARRIER REEF

A diverse range of habitats

As the Great Barrier Reef covers such a vast area, there are many habitats that constitute it, feed into it or otherwise influence it. It is this diversity that makes coral reefs, along with rainforests, the most biodiverse ecosystems on the planet. In this chapter we will travel eastwards from the ridgeline of the Queensland watershed down the rivers and streams, into the estuaries and their associated mangroves, mudflats, sand flats and seagrass meadows, onto seafloor gardens and *Halimeda* meadows leading out to and among the reefs. Then we will explore a sample of typical coral reef habitats before descending the edge of the continental shelf into the abyss of the Queensland Trench.

As we explore these habitats, we will look at the overall environment, not the smaller-scale habitats that occur within them. In any of these habitats every surface is covered or embedded with life— from the bacteria and fungi at the microscopic scale through foraminferans, lace corals (bryozoans), algae, small crustaceans and worms of many kinds, up to large coral heads, which provide habitats for thousands of other organisms.

On the Great Barrier Reef, there are habitats within habitats, rather like Russian dolls. As sharks cruise entire reefs, a clown- or anemonefish may confine itself to a square metre of habitat while a coral polyp may occupy a square millimetre. The Great Barrier Reef Marine Park Authority

(GBRMPA) has defined at least seventy 'bioregions'—broad-scale habitats—but these do not include Torres Strait. Of these, thirty are reefal and forty non-reefal. Each is defined by its plant and animal life and its physical characteristics, such as reef types, stages of growth, shelf depths and lagoons.

It is likely that the Great Barrier Reef was in its prime about 5500 years ago, when the reefs were all reaching their peak in coral cover and diversity, and sea levels were about 2 m (6½ ft) higher. These days, seagrass, shoals and sandy or muddy seabeds (up to 200 m/656 ft deep) comprise 61 per cent of the Great Barrier Reef Region, whereas the thirty bioregions of coral reefs comprise 7 per cent.

Under the present Great Barrier Reef there are several fossilised layers of older coral reef systems that represent the last 500,000 years. In that time four glaciation events have occurred, creating low sea levels, exposing the entire Queensland continental shelf and any reefs on it to terrestrial erosion, sedimentation and runoff.

About 12,000 years ago the shelf began to be submerged again, and new fields of algae formed banks and ridges from Cooktown to Torres Strait.

Coral reef growth began about 18,000 years ago, reaching the present height after 4000 years. The flow of rivers across the shelf during low sea-stands would also have contributed to the shapes of some of the reefs you can see today.

Previous spread: The clownfish is one of the few species of fish that can live with a certain type of anemone without being stung by its tentacles. For more information on their symbiotic relationship, see page 71.

Opposite: Whitsunday Island, where tropical rainforest helps to regulate the flow of water and sediment into the sea and onto the Great Barrier Reef.

Cape York Peninsula

Wet Tropics

Brigalow Belt

Central Queensland Coast

Southeastern Queensland

Water moving onto the continental shelf caused it to sink so quickly in several sections of the Great Barrier Reef that reef growth could not keep up; however, in other sections the shelf rose. This warping effect eroded the surfaces of some reefs. You can see these different forms of reef throughout the province.

In addition, there are five mainland bioregions adjacent to the Great Barrier Reef, each with sub-regions that are determined by mudflats, soil type, vegetation and land use.

These bioregions are:
- Cape York Peninsula, a large area of hills and broad alluvial plains, with rainforest environ-ments found along the coast;
- the Wet Tropics, south of Cape York, which is a narrow coastal floodplain cleared for sugar-cane, bananas and urbanisation, flanked by steep mountains covered in some of the most ancient rainforest on the planet;
- the Brigalow Belt, further south, which includes the Whitsunday, Lindeman and Cumberland island groups;
- the Central Queensland Coast—a region of lowlands, hills and ranges—which experiences

a high rainfall, with 50–60 per cent of the total rainfall occurring between January and March; savannah woodlands and semi-deciduous forests characterise the lower altitudes of this bioregion while rainforest and tall eucalypt forests repre-sent the higher altitudes; and, finally
- Southeastern Queensland, which includes the World Heritage-listed Fraser Island; it has one of Australia's highest rates of population growth, and supports subtropical rainforests and coastal heathlands of significance.

The mainland habitats are determined by their climate and weather, soils, location (in relation to height above sea level), rain shadow effects and also human activity. Since the mid-1800s, human activity has had a major effect on the quality of fresh water as a result of sediments from eroded grazing country as well as nutrients and pesticides from agriculture, mining and urban development. Since the early 2000s there has been a much clearer understanding of the severity of the situation, which has led to substantial investment by government and industry to 'halt and reverse the decline' in water quality.

Previous spread: High cliffs near Cape Bedford, in the Cape York Peninsula bioregion, have been sculpted by wave action over thousands of years.

Above: The five bioregions of the Great Barrier Reef.

Opposite: Mossman Gorge in Daintree National Park, a World Heritage Area in Queensland, is in the Wet Tropics bioregion.

Opposite: The view from Cook's Lookout on Hayman Island in the Whitsunday Group, part of the Brigalow Belt bioregion.

Above: A billabong near Proserpine in the Central Queensland coast bioregion.

Left: An aerial view of Lake McKenzie, one of a hundred freshwater lakes on Fraser Island in the Southeastern Queensland bioregion.

The waterways of the Reef

Every activity that occurs in the watersheds on the eastern side of the Great Dividing Range, which extends down the entire east coast of Australia, has the potential to influence ecosystems beyond the Great Barrier Reef. The characteristics of the different bioregions—including topography, basic rock types, climate, vegetation and human use—are reflected in the nature of the rivers and streams. The pattern of water flow is highly seasonal, with strong flows and floods in the wet summer or monsoonal season, and reduced or even non-existent flow in the dry winter season.

Above: Hill Inlet at the northern end of Whitehaven Beach on Whitsunday Island, an intertidal area where mangroves help stabilise the shifting sands, provides habitats for a diverse range of species, including shore and migratory birds.

Rivers naturally carry sediment and nutrients that are eroded from the landscape. These materials contribute to the growth of deltas, floodplains and beaches, and also to the increased quantity of nutrients in coastal systems.

As part of their breeding cycle, several species of fish and prawns (shrimp) make the journey from the sea to deep inland and back again, relying on high water quality throughout the system. Scientists are gradually understanding how important it is to ensure that no stage in this journey is interrupted by poor water quality, weed growth, culverts or dams.

The extensive grazing areas of the drier country on the mainland contribute enormous amounts of sediment during wet season floods as over-grazed land and riverbanks are eroded. Meanwhile, the cultivated areas, especially on floodplains, contribute huge amounts of nutrients from pesticides and excessive applications of fertiliser. Both mining activities and port dredging contribute sediments and, in some cases, toxic substances to waterways, while urban development can be the source of large amounts of nutrients, pesticides and various types of organic material entering the system. Again, the

major inputs occur during floods, although it is likely that a steady input during low flows also affects coastal systems. It is this constant addition of materials that has the largest effect on ecosystems.

The Australian Institute of Marine Science's extensive program of coral coring—exploring the history of reefs across the continental shelf—found that, even well out onto the shelf, the reefs are inundated with fresh water associated with annual cyclonic or monsoonal floods.

Practices such as clearing rainforest to create farming land, towns, cities and tourist resorts along the coast make the Great Barrier Reef vulnerable to polluted runoff.

Under ultra-violet light, different bands—rather like growth rings in trees—can be seen in the cores of corals. These are a result of the deposit of humic substances from decaying vegetation on the land. Because of the longevity of many corals, some of the cores recorded seasonal floods several hundred years ago, allowing for observations on the effects of land clearing, mining and agriculture.

Since the pollution of Great Barrier Reef waters has been identified as a major issue, state and federal agencies have been working with local councils, regional resource management groups and mining and agricultural bodies to help them minimise their impact on the environment.

Left: The port of Gladstone, the site of a power station, a bauxite refinery, coal terminals and an alumina refinery, is a jump-off point for the Capricorn and Bunker Group. To maintain its viability, it must be dredged.

Left: The mudskipper, an amphibious fish that uses its pectoral fins to walk on land, lives on intertidal mudflats.

Opposite: A stilt mangrove, where fiddler crabs and mud whelks eat mud, producing waste that is eaten by shrimp, and so on, up the food chain.

Mangroves

About half the world's mangrove species—salt-tolerant trees and shrubs—cover more than 4000 square km (1544 square mi) of Queensland's coast, and there are thousands more hectares of mangroves in Torres Strait and New Guinea.

Mangroves are extremely important. They protect the coast by acting as a buffer against storm-driven waves. They also help capture silt runoff that might otherwise smother important marine communities offshore; the captured silt helps to promote the growth of more mangroves. Captured along with the silt is an abundance of biological material, which settles before being broken down by bacteria and fungi; the bacterial numbers in the Queensland mangroves are higher than in any other muds in the world. These microbes are eaten by small animals such as crabs and snails, which in turn provide food for many species that live permanently in the mangrove ecosystem, using it as a nursery area for their young.

The mangroves also provide feeding and breeding habitats for many large fish species. Some experts estimate that more than 75 per cent of the fish caught in Queensland waters rely on mangroves as part of their life cycle.

Finally, mangroves provide habitat for a range of terrestrial or semi-terrestrial insects, birds and reptiles that live in a forest food web or, in the case of many birds, feast off such creatures as worms, mussels and prawns (shrimp) on the mudflats. Capping off this food web, which maps the connections between plants and animals that rely on each other for survival, is the the estuarine crocodile (see pages 38–9 and 130).

Indigenous people of Australia and Asia have long used mangroves for food, firewood, building material and medicinal purposes. The richest of these forests can be found at river mouths with good sandy and muddy substrates. The Reef coast has been recognised as the origin of mangroves and their many associated plants, so they are a vital step in the evolution of plants and coastal ecosystems as well as the reefs themselves.

Mudflats

Mud accumulates off river mouths, among mangroves and out to sea between the reefs. In general, intertidal mudflats—where a vast array of specialised plants and animals thrive—are more stable than sand flats. On the mudflats you can see burrowing worms of all types, crabs, walking fish (or mudskippers), mangrove snakes and the very rich flora and fauna at the base of the food chain. You can also see spirals of mud on the surface of the mudflats, formed by a worm that passes mud through its digestive system in order to extract any microscopic sustenance. This is one of the many animals that use micro-organisms for food.

Male fiddler crabs have one oversized claw, which they use in courtship and territorial rituals. As they feed on detritus, they aerate the surface of the sand or mud, leaving small sediment balls near the entrance to their burrows.

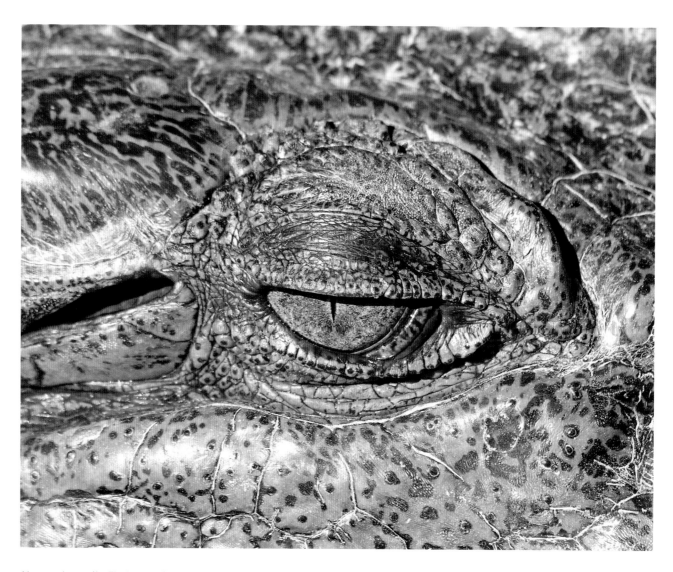

Above and opposite: The largest of all living reptiles, the saltwater or estuarine crocodile is adapted to both freshwater and salt water, so it can live in estuaries, swamps, creeks, rivers and the sea.

Opposite: The green sea turtle's jaw is finely serrated for eating seagrass (pictured), algae and seajellies.

Right: As the sand bubbler crab forages in beach sand for food, it forms tiny balls of sand, which will be washed away by the next high tide. Can you spot the crab in this photograph?

Sand flats and beaches

Massive amounts of sediment pour out of river mouths onto the Reef every year. The finer sediments make up mudflats or are suspended in the water column until they combine with other particles and sink to the sea floor, often far out to sea. Every sand flat or beach is rich in life, even if it is quite mobile; beaches on the leeward side of coral cays swing like a tail as the winds change from the prevailing mid-year southeasterlies to the summer northerlies.

Some of the most intriguing life to be found in this habitat are the miniature interstitial life forms—fauna and flora that thrive between the sand grains and provide food for foraging crabs, birds and worms. Sand ridges and sea-floor sand communities between reefs are also rich in bizarre life forms. Often burrowing worms feeding on the interstitial life send up spirals of sand, while the burrowing ghost and sand bubbler crabs will also create piles of different coloured sand near their burrows, indicating the various sources of sand deposited below the surface.

Seagrass meadows

In the Great Barrier Reef Region, there are more than 6000 square km (2317 square mi) of seagrass beds, with Torres Strait areas adding thousands more. Their coverage fluctuates annually, especially in southern areas where river outflows are stressing the systems. These thick, lush meadows, which seem almost impenetrable, can grow up to 50 cm (20 in) deep, but they can also grow very sparsely across sand flats or mudflats in less than ideal conditions.

As with every other surface to be found in Great Barrier Reef waters, seagrasses tend to be heavily colonised by many other small organisms, such as algae, forams (small single-celled animals), bacteria, fungi and prawns (shrimp). In addition to this fabulous food source, for many animals and their larvae, seagrasses also provide protected nursery areas for the young of many species.

Fast Fact

Seagrasses are flowering plants that have fully adapted to life under the sea. They flower once a year, and their pollen, which floats on the current, enables them to fertilise the female plants nearby.

41

'Sea cows'

The iconic seagrass dweller is the dugong, a large
docile mammal that grazes on seagrass (much like
cattle on land graze on grass); divers can hear them
crunching their way across the meadow. The numbers
of these very shy mammals, which grow up to 3 m
(10 ft) long and regularly come up to the surface to
breathe, have plummeted so much that they are now
on the list of endangered species. Living in herds of
up to 100 or more, they leave feeding trails about
25 cm (10 in) wide, which can be visible from the air.
(For more information on dugongs, see also page 133.)

Previous spread: Whitehaven
Beach, Whitsunday Island,
where sand pours out of the
river mouth at Hill Inlet.

Above: The dugong feeds
exclusively on seagrass. Its
down-turned snout is specially
adapted for grazing on, and
uprooting, the vegetation (as
seen in the above image).

Right: Looking a little like flowerless stems, garden eels poke their heads out of their burrows on the sea floor, where they feed on plankton.

Far right: The horned sea star uses its dark protuberances, which look like chocolate chips, to scare off predators. Its preferred habitat is seagrass or coral sand on the sea floor.

The success of seagrass meadows relies on a delicate balance—the right amount of silt carries nutrients that can aid growth, but too much may smother them, cutting out the light essential for growth, or decreasing the depth to a low tide exposure that kills off the plants. Their roots help stabilise the sediments that are washed out to sea, and this in turn may eventually create shallow sea floors suitable for mangrove colonisation.

Halimeda bioherms

Imagine diving down to see long underwater dunes of one species of algae, *Halimeda*, found on the reef between Cooktown and Torres Strait. The living plants cover the surface of the dunes, but beneath them are up to 18 m (59 ft) of their skeletal calcium carbonate remains. These mounds, which cover more than 5000 square km (1930 square mi) of sea floor, are maintained by jets of cold and nutrient-rich waters that surge up from the depths of the ocean onto the continental shelf under the warmer waters. The *Halimeda* bioherms provide habitats and grazing opportunities for many species, especially those in their juvenile stages.

Sea-floor communities

As you move out into the deeper waters beyond the seagrass meadows, you come to the areas between the reefs and shoals, which can be either continental rock or coral reef in origin. These are very important in the migration of growing fish and crustaceans. Often these inter-reefal sea floors appear almost devoid of life, especially when viewed from a distance or on the screen of a fishing boat's sonar. However, if you dive down, or send down a remote camera, many different pictures emerge.

Any piece of hard substrate, such as an old shell or coral skeleton, has a rich collection of life both on and around it, and sheltering within will be worms, crabs, prawns (shrimp) and fish. This is why small patches between the reefs and the mainland, and among the reefs themselves, can be so important. Meanwhile the sea floors provide habitat for flat fish and a host of invertebrates, including sea stars, heart urchins, prawns (shrimp) and crabs.

The allure of wreck dives

A significant example of a sea-floor habitat is the wreck of the SS *Yongala*, a coastal steamer that sank near Townsville in 1911. Often described as one of the best wreck dives in the world, it features a superb range of life, from algae, soft corals, hard reef-building corals and diverse communities of massive oysters, worms, snails, prawns (shrimp) and sea stars to top predators such as Queensland groupers the size of a small car. Schools of trevally, kingfish, sharks and black cow-tailed rays cruise constantly around the wreck.

Right: A vast plankton bloom on the Great Barrier Reef.

Inter-reefal waters

In the dry season, the coastal waters of the Great Barrier Reef can be clear, but after the wet season there may be a rich soup of runoff silts, chemicals, muds and nutrients. Under these conditions a 'bloom' or explosion of algal populations such as *Trichodesmium* can occur. These blooms add a massive amount of biomass to the system as food for the bottom of the food chain.

Further away from land, the water is generally much clearer for a longer period of the year until, beyond the edge of the continental shelf, it becomes the deep azure of the ocean. From a land lookout or an aircraft, it is common to see the meeting of the edges of the two water masses as a wall of muddy water meeting a wall of clear blue water; their different chemical and physical characteristics will not mix. It is here that you can sometimes see massive blooms of algae, as one water mass supplies the other water mass with nutrients or gases in which it is deficient. The algae in turn attract grazing zooplankton, which may draw lines of feeding fish and manta rays along the aptly named 'slick line', where the water can be frothy, smooth or thrashing with life.

The fish found in inter-reefal waters tend to be the fast swimmers—such as queenfish, trevally, sailfish, marlin, mackerel and tuna—which flash past as they hunt smaller fish species. Here you can also see whales, dolphins, turtles and sea snakes, as they must all come regularly to the surface to breathe.

Above: Fast-swimming marlin can reach speeds of up to 110 km (68 mi) per hour, it is common to see these fast-swimmers in inter-reefal waters.

Opposite: The dwarf minke whale was not recognised as a separate minke species until the 1980s. This 'gulper' feeder gulps large volumes of water, trapping fish and krill, shrimp-like cristaceans, behind a row of fine bristles, called baleen plates.

Right: A *Pisonia* forest on Heron Island, a coral cay off the southern coast of Queensland.

Islands on the Great Barrier Reef

There are three main types of islands on the Reef—continental, rocky or mainland islands; coral sand cays; and coral rubble cays.

Continental, rocky or mainland islands

The remnants of ancient land-building processes, these islands are essentially part of the mainland, joined to it by the continental shelf underneath. Some are no more than a few rocks sticking above the surface, while others are thousands of hectares in area. Most are circled by fringing reefs (see page 10), many of which are adapted to withstand the sediments washed off the island as well as the low light conditions of the silty waters. There are tourist resorts on many of these islands.

Coral sand cays

These islands range from small ephemeral sand banks to large islands covered in rich vegetation, and the sand of some cays contains a very high percentage of foram shells. In the Capricorn and Bunker Group of islands and reefs to the south,

cays are covered with strandline plants at the high tide line and above, into an intermediate plant line—usually spinifex or couch grasses, goat's foot convolvulus vines and casuarinas (she-oaks)—and then into *Pisonia* forests. Rich rainforest grows on some of the northern cays, such as Green and East Hope islands, but the vegetation varies a great deal between the coral sand cays; the overwash of big storms and tides keeps some cays bare, or growing only grasses. There are resorts on five of these cays, and in Torres Strait several cays support villages of Torres Strait Islander people.

Coral rubble cays

Rubble banks—made up of smashed up corals, clam shells and other shell and algal remains—can be found on many reefs. Usually heavy seas move them around, from Low Isles northwards into Torres Strait. The rubble cays in the north usually feature rich mangrove communities in relatively clear water. Clams, sponges, algae and seagrasses live on the seabeds between them, while corals and sponges grow on their stilt roots or stems.

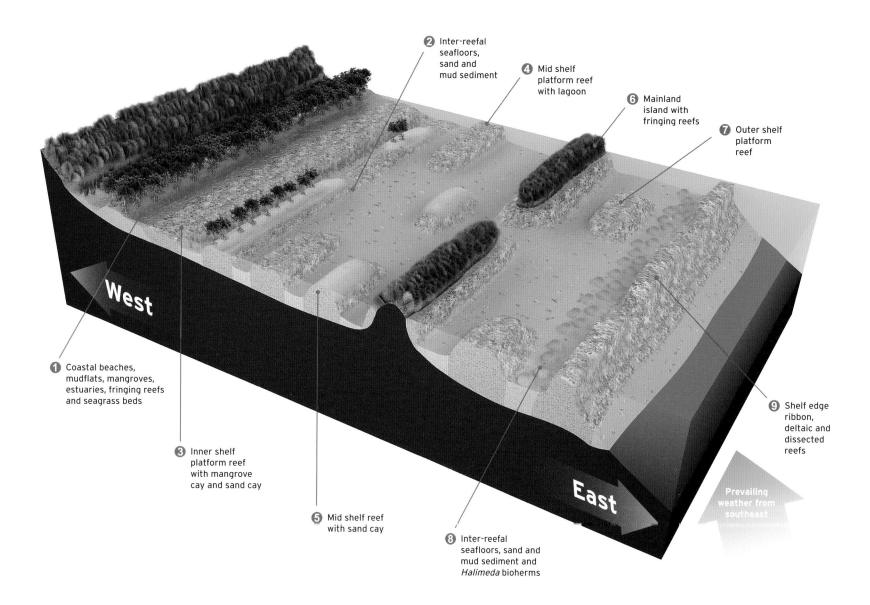

2 Inter-reefal seafloors, sand and mud sediment

4 Mid shelf platform reef with lagoon

6 Mainland island with fringing reefs

7 Outer shelf platform reef

West

1 Coastal beaches, mudflats, mangroves, estuaries, fringing reefs and seagrass beds

3 Inner shelf platform reef with mangrove cay and sand cay

5 Mid shelf reef with sand cay

East

9 Shelf edge ribbon, deltaic and dissected reefs

8 Inter-reefal seafloors, sand and mud sediment and *Halimeda* bioherms

Prevailing weather from southeast

Coral reef habitats

A coral reef typically features a wide range of habitats, enhanced by both its three-dimensional architecture and its fine-scale variation in structure, caused by different coral and algal species, broken corals, channels and currents.

As you move east towards the edge of the continental shelf, the first indication of a reef is a sand slope, often with rubble or living coral ridges, which are usually very fragile on this lee side of the reef. In protected, shallower waters, there are thriving, densely populated communities of coral and associated fish. Towards the reef top, the corals become more robust; on the top itself the colonies are stunted due to wave and current action.

Boulders, scattered by cyclones and storms along the edge of the reef tops, provide protection for a myriad of life forms. Some of these boulders are as big as small cars, but usually they are less than 1 m (3 ft) across. It is here you will also find small gutters and pools like mini-aquariums. This is great reef-walking country best explored with a guide.

If there is a coral cay on the reef, then it is usually on this back reef area where the waves wrap around the reef to meet and drop any sediment they have picked off the reef top. Towards the edge of the lagoon, the back reef usually drops vertically to the lagoon floor. These walls are great for snorkellers, who may see coral gardens on the floor below, extending right across

Above: This diagram is a representation of the main geological features of a reef, showing where the different elements might be found in relation to each other. *Image source: Andrew McWhae.*

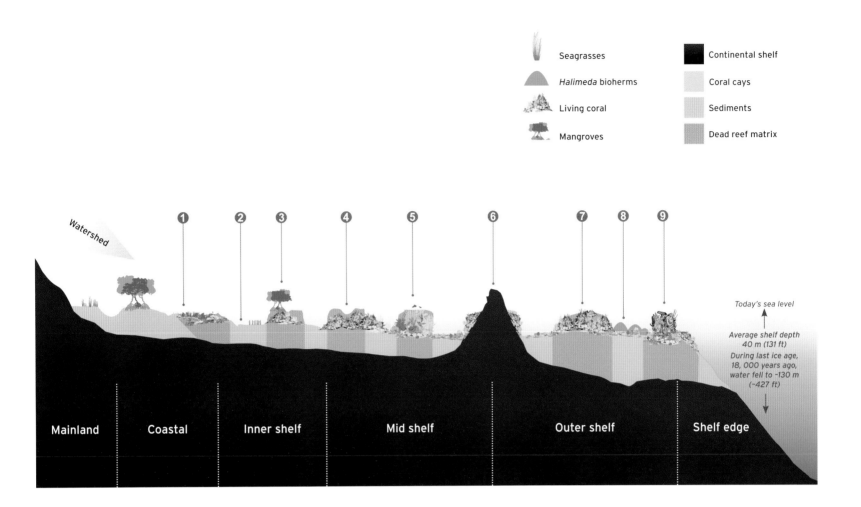

Seagrasses

Halimeda bioherms

Living coral

Mangroves

Continental shelf

Coral cays

Sediments

Dead reef matrix

Watershed

① ② ③ ④ ⑤ ⑥ ⑦ ⑧ ⑨

Today's sea level

Average shelf depth 40 m (131 ft) During last ice age, 18, 000 years ago, water fell to -130 m (-427 ft)

Mainland | **Coastal** | **Inner shelf** | **Mid shelf** | **Outer shelf** | **Shelf edge**

Above: This is a cross-section representation of the 3D diagram on the facing page. *Image source: Len Zell.*

the lagoon and often punctuated by isolated coral heads or bommies. Some reef lagoons have lacework patterns of reef growth, but older lagoons will have a flat sandy floor. Lagoon edges closer to the reef front tend to be patchy coral heads with sand 'streams' in between. This sand has been formed by smashed corals and grazing fish, such as the bump-head parrotfish, which literally crushes the skeletons as it eats the algae, then defecates the waste as sand.

The top of the reef on the weather side of the reef is usually covered with small robust colonies on the lagoon side, then grades into a flatter algal/coral mix, often known as the reef pavement, in the reef crest zone. Sometimes this pavement is made up of coralline algae, corals or turf algae, with mussels

growing within it. As the water deepens over the crest onto the reef's upper slope, the corals become less robust but gradually larger. The middle slope has more of the larger plate corals, leading you into the lower slope where they may be several metres across.

As you drop deeper below the lower slope, you begin to enter the low light zone where there is less coral and algal growth. Here the soft coral fans and other filter feeders are more common. On the reefs on the outer edge of the continental shelf there is a series of terraces, indicating the lower sea levels of times past.

The Queensland Trench

At the edge of the continental shelf and the outer Great Barrier Reef, the light levels rapidly decrease as the sea bottom slopes steeply into the depths, where different biological zones can be found. The light-reliant algae and reef-building hard corals disappear, and the filter and detrital feeders take over, allowing a greater number of soft corals and other animals to become predominant.

Deep in the Queensland Trench, discovered when more capable depth-sounding equipment was developed, the sea floor is covered with fine mud, a rich ooze of decaying life that has drifted down from the surface. Bacteria as well as many specialised animals, such as sea stars, thrive on this nutritious food supply.

These deep waters, at the 200 m (656 ft) deep line, attract big-game fishers who like to try their luck on blue marlin, black marlin and sailfish, which feed on the smaller species, such as mackerel and dart, thriving in this productive reef-edge zone.

Above: Between Cormorant Reef (in the foreground) and Ribbon No 10 Reef is Cormorant Pass, where divers can access Cod Hole, a renowned diving site in the Coral Sea.

Opposite: Wide ribbon reefs divide the continental shelf from the deep oceanic waters of the Queensland Trench.

3

A DAY IN THE LIFE OF THE REEF

The Great Barrier Reef at noon

Coral reefs are affected by many factors—the rhythms of tides, moon phases, oceanic currents and wave action as well as sunlight, storms and cyclones, water temperature, salinity, carbon dioxide and oxygen levels, and food, nutrients and chemicals in the passing waters.

We begin our day on the Reef at noon in summer. It's hot and humid, and beneath us are clear, calm waters hiding a thriving reef ecosystem. At this time of day the reef-building corals are all in the 'farming' phase. The coral animals, or polyps, must maximise their surface area so the colourful algae, called zooxanthellae, which live in the coral, can absorb light and process it with the carbon dioxide, phosphate and nitrate wastes from the coral colony. In exchange, the corals receive oxygen, sugars and protein, the byproducts of the algae's photosynthesis.

As a result of this symbiotic process, the polyps produce waste—limestone in a porous crystalline form. Just as we put our rubbish out, so do the coral polyps, except they lay it down in the most intricate of patterns—a different one for each species. These form the coral skeleton, or reef.

Corals are vulnerable to species that can reach them in their limey cups. The beaked butterfly fish, for example, feed on both the coral polyps and the small animals living among them, they do this with their very small mouth which is on the end of its long nose. Meanwhile the parrotfish and the bumphead parrotfish swim in and bite off whole hunks of coral to get at the algae—you can hear them crunching their way across the reef top, especially on the rising tide, when they swim up from deeper waters. They excrete sand, so they play an important part in the growth and erosion of the reef system.

The other marine creatures seem relaxed, as if they are affected by the hot, humid conditions. Fish cruise around while soft corals wave their frond or whip shapes in the passing current, catching any food particles. The buried sea cucumber pokes its feathery arms above the sandy sea floor, looking for food, and crinoids, or feather stars, also send out their arms in search of prey.

Fast Fact

Coral reefs are formed by polyps, small organisms with a hard limestone skeleton at their base. They attach themselves to a rock, then divide thousands of times as they form a colony. A reef is formed by many colonies joined together.

Previous spread: A coral outcrop maximises sunlight during the 'farming phase'. Coral polyps live with algae called zooxanthellae in a symbiotic, or mutually beneficial, relationship.

Opposite: On the Great Barrier Reef a rich world of amazingly diverse life is in constant motion. Here orange fairy basslets feed on plankton as they drift past feather stars.

Above: The beaked coralfish, which grows to 20 cm (8 in) long, uses its long snout to pick out inverts from within the reef.

Above left: A Maori wrasse, or humphead wrasse, at the Cod Hole (see page 54). This species of wrasse feeds on a variety of molluscs, fish, sea urchins, crustaceans and other invertebrates.

Above: Bumphead parrotfish feature an almost vertical forehead and also large blue-green tooth plates.

Right: A blue-streak cleaner wrasse removes parasites and dead skin from a moray eel.

Opposite: The prawn-killing mantis shrimp, which can perceive both depth and three dimensions with only one of its eyes, at the mouth of its burrow. It often waits for dark before it goes hunting.

The soft corals and other filter feeders use a variety of capture and kill techniques to satisfy their hunger. The prawn-killing mantis shrimp lurks at the mouth of its burrow, then demonstrates the fastest move in the animal kingdom as it spears its prey (see also page 152). A goatfish moves across the sand, wriggling the two chemosensory barbels or 'whiskers' on its chin into the sand, quickly burrowing out any prey it detects. Wrasse will follow, capturing any other creatures the goatfish may disturb.

'Cleaner stations'

Manta rays and other species float above a coral head, apparently in a dream-like state, as small cleaner wrasse dart all over their bodies, plucking off parasites or dead skin. Sometimes the sabre-toothed blennie, which is almost identical to the cleaner wrasse, will cruise out and take a bite from a fish, making it dart off. These 'cleaner stations', always a popular spot for the local animals, can be found all over every reef.

Out in the deeper water, on the flat sandy floors adjacent to the reefs, it is common to see hundreds of garden eels—long worm-like fish with about 60 cm (2 ft) of their bodies out of their burrows—swaying with the current, waiting for passing food. One quick move and they will all disappear, only to re-emerge as soon as the threat has passed on.

The aptly named Christmas-tree worm, which is renowned for its amazing range of bright colours, lives in a tube in a coral head. Whenever it is disturbed, this delicate creature will draw back its pair of feathery spiral-shaped cones into the tube, slamming a cap tightly over them. These worms are known to form dense colonies, especially on kidney coral heads.

The giant clam is spectacular. Its mantle, which is 50 cm (20 in) wide when the shell is fully relaxed and 'farming' (see page 59), can be all the colours of the rainbow. Like the corals, giant clams have zooxanthellae in their tissues, so they are farmers by day and filter feeders on small animals by night. There are many species of bivalves on the Great Barrier Reef. Some use both chemical and physical erosion to burrow into the coral (see page 116), while others live freely on the sea floor, swimming about by squirting water from between their shells.

Opposite: Looking like festive decorations, Christmas-tree worms use the feathery tentacles on their colourful spirals to capture prey and transport it to their mouths. As they also use these tentacles—or radioles—to breathe, they are called 'gills'.

Above: Some giant clams reach a metre (3 ft) in length, with each of the two shells —or valves—weighing 100 kg (200 lb).

Camouflaged feeders

The Reef is home to every form of camouflage and
feeding technique imaginable. Occasionally part
of the sea floor will seem to erupt as a stonefish
swallows a passing fish, or the red and white lionfish,
apparently asleep, will dart out from its crevice and
gulp down another fish. The heavily camouflaged
stonefish looks like an algae-covered rock lying on
the sea floor. It shares its habitat with sole, which
also erupts from the sand to catch prey.

The decorator crab sticks old bits of sponge
and algae onto its body; sometimes it will even place
a few small anemones on the front of its shell to help
ward off predators. Some small octopi camouflage
themselves by changing their shape to resemble that
of a hermit crab, while the seahorses just rock back
and forth, looking like harmless floating objects,
until they suddenly snap up food.

Above left: The stonefish, the
most venomous fish on Earth,
has venom stored in the base
of all its spines and can stay
out of the water for up to
24 hours, making it a hazard
for reef-walkers.

Above: A decorator crab's shell
is covered with hooks, allowing
it to camouflage itself with
algae, sponges and seaweed.

Opposite: With its spiky and
venomous fin rays and ability
to alter its centre of gravity,
the lionfish is a precision hunter.

As sea cucumbers crawl along the sandy sea floor or among the corals, up to thirty feathery feeding tentacles pick up sand, bacteria and food materials, which pass through their guts, leaving behind a mucus-coated rope of faeces and clean sand. Their role as 'vacuum cleaners of the sea' is very important in the reef ecosystem.

If you pick one up and look at its end, you'll see the five rows of tube feet running the length of its body—just like the five arms of its relative, the sea star, only grossly elongated.

The sea cucumber breathes by pumping water in and out of its anus. Sometimes, towards night-time, a pearl fish will sense the opening of the anus as the sea cucumber pumps out water and will dart into the safety of its host's gut for the night. If necessary, the pearl fish can even use its tail to encourage the sea cucumber to 'exhale'.

Previous spread: Schooling yellow-striped goatfish and bigeye sea perch hug a reef.

Above left: A pearl fish surveys the terrain from the safety of the sea cucumber's anus, where it feeds on the nutrients passing in and out of its host.

Above: An orange clownfish in the tentacles of its host— a magnificent sea anemone. As the clownfish swims around, it creates water movement around the anemone, making it easier for the cnidarian to feed.

Opposite: An emperor shrimp changes its colour pattern to match its host but you can identify one by its purple pincers and legs. This one is riding on a sea cucumber.

Mutual dependence

On the reef top and in the lagoons you'll see many examples of animals and plants living together in some form of commensal or symbiotic relationship. Commensals are creatures that live off another without harming or benefiting it, unlike parasitic molluscs—true parasites—which burrow into sea cucumbers to eat their innards.

If you stay still long enough, you'll see a small goby, constantly in contact with the tip of a shrimp's antenna, emerge from a hole in the sand of the sea floor. If the goby remains relaxed and still, the shrimp, which does not see as well as the goby, will begin bulldozing out their communal burrow.

The wonderful clownfish and anemones can be found living together in almost all reef habitats. The clownfish cleans the anemone, which is usually spread out on the surface of the reef, and provides food in the form of waste. The clownfish also lays its eggs under the anemone for protection, but when it is feeding or protecting itself, the flower-like cnidarian will curl up into a ball, exposing the eggs, which will then be eaten very quickly by any keen-eyed wrasse in the area.

The spectacular emperor shrimp can usually be found on the long feathermouth—a long, thin transparent cousin of the sea cucumber—or the Spanish dancer, the most colourful nudibranch of all. This shrimp seems to hitch a ride on its host, keeping it free of parasites and also helping itself to any spare food from the host's mouth. Both the nudibranch and the feathermouth are unpleasant to eat, thus offering the shrimp some protection.

It's late afternoon and suddenly a small female surgeonfish bursts out of a group towards the surface, releases its eggs and dashes back to the group. Meanwhile, several males quickly follow her to the surface, release their sperm near her eggs in bursts, like little clouds of smoke, then also dash back down. The school resumes its casual cruising until the next female bursts upwards.

At dusk

As evening approaches, the underwater sounds change, and the reef becomes much noisier as the daytime animals begin to retreat to their sleeping places. A little later, the night-time species will emerge—some to forage all night, others to feed at dusk and dawn only. This 'change of shifts' is a favourite attraction for many divers. The small coris will seem to dive-bomb a patch of sand and disappear as it spends the night, like many other daytime species, buried.

With some parrotfish species, a pair will spiral towards the surface to release their eggs and sperm together in a cloud of gametes (reproductive cells) before dashing back to the protection of the reef. The water becomes a little murky as more and more gametes are released.

At this time of day the cruising high-speed fish such as trevally will burst out of the gloom into schooling balls of baitfish near coral heads, while lionfish will drift among the baitfish and snap one up every now and then.

Octopi will become active, moving from one hide to the next. Occasionally they will turn pure white and cover a small coral head to confuse the fish or crab within, who thinks it can still see daylight and tries to escape the probing tentacle, only to become the octopus' next meal.

Night feeders

At night the corals become carnivores by pumping out their tentacles and using them to capture the zooplankton that rise up from the sea floor. As a tentacle makes contact with one of these small animals, the coral uses stinging capsules to capture and paralyse its prey, then folds it into its mouth, where it is digested. The coral ejects any large pieces of waste from its mouth, but it keeps the chemical wastes to feed the zooxanthellae during the farming phase in daylight hours (see page 59).

During the night, rays hunt the sands. When a micro-electric current from the breath or twitch of a buried animal is detected, it spurts a jet of water onto the spot and captures the hidden mollusc, crab or fish.

Sea snakes and sharks also hunt at night, and both look among the corals for sleeping fish.

Fast Fact

A feeding white-tip shark, one of the many species of shark that do not have to keep swimming to stay alive, will keep its head stuck in a cave until it has eaten its prey so it won't have to share food with its fellows.

Opposite: The highly venomous olive sea snake hides among coral during the day and feeds at night.

Several species of shrimp, which prefer to hide in dark crevices during the day, usually clean fish at night, performing a fascinating series of dances on any fish that 'parks' in the right spot.

The clown shrimp is a fierce predator which uses its claws to pierce the skin of a crown-of-thorns sea star before eating its flesh.

The basket star may live in the same place all its life, although it can move around. It unfolds its delicate fronds from a crevice in the coral then casts its net of many-branched arms, which can span 2 m (6½ ft), across the current to feed. It then collapses one arm at a time into its mouth and scrapes off any food.

Previous spread: A manta ray forages for plankton with a school of golden trevally as pilotfish ride the manta's pressure wave. Like other members of the shark family, mantas must keep swimming in order to breathe.

Above: At night, anchored to a soft coral, a basket star uses its arms to feed on plankton.

Right: An *Acropora* coral sets and releases egg bundles into the water column.

Spawning at night

Once a year, usually about the fifth night after the first or second full moon in summer, most species of coral have amassed their eggs and sperm into bundles in their gut cavity, waiting for night.

As the sea darkens, many of the corals begin to bulge at the mouth with pink, yellow, white or orange as they prepare their egg and sperm bundles for ejection. Once all the conditions—such as lunar cycle, day length, tide height, temperature and salinity—are right, the corals begin to release their gametes. Most are hermaphrodites, which release their eggs and sperm separately, while some are monosexual—you can see the males releasing their smoke-like sperm while the females release bundles or even single eggs into the sea in clouds of red, yellow, orange and almost white. All rise slowly to the surface, where the process of fertilisation begins. This mass spawning process has been called an 'upside down snowstorm'.

Banded brittle stars, 50 cm (20 in) across, are also spawning. The males are inside a branching coral colony, emitting their sperm so that it looks as if the coral itself is smoking. Standing up on two of her five arms, the female rapidly whips the other three backwards and forwards as she releases a steady stream of individual red eggs into the water.

Sea cucumbers, not wanting to miss the party, stand up on about a third of their body length. With two-thirds of their bodies vertical and their 'heads' bent horizontal, they too begin to sway gently back and forth as the females release their red eggs and the males release a steady stream of grey sperm from the genital pore on their heads. The sperm and eggs float to the surface.

Female crown-of-thorns sea stars will release up to 250 million eggs in one year, and many other species cast adrift large numbers of eggs and sperm. We have no idea what their survival rate is, as so many factors affect their success. Probably the most important one is to be able to dodge the walls and carpets of mouths that confront them on any reef surface and then find a spot that is just right for settlement—a very difficult task!

Worms of many species zoom up to the surface to drop whole sections of their bodies, which break up into gamete masses, allowing fertilisation to occur. Many other groups of species now join in this once a year opportunity, dumping their gametes into the water column.

Life cycle of a polyp

Planulae larvae form after the fertilised eggs rapidly divide into small cigar-shaped, cilia-coated mobile animals that will either swim back down to the reef or stay afloat in the water for up to 100 days before settling. Once settled, they will each form one new coral polyp, then divide into two, then four, eight, sixteen and so on, until a new colony is formed. Their limestone skeletons begin to develop as soon as they start farming the single-celled algae (zooxanthellae) in their tissues (see also page 59).

The long survival time for some planula species allows widespread distribution, but others may be limited due to their larvae's ability to survive. If larvae attach to a piece of floating debris such as an old tree or pumice from volcanic action (see right), they may grow into a colony that is carried right across the ocean, releasing their gametes each year—or each month for some species—over a very wide area. Scientists have found hard and soft corals, fish, crabs, worms and countless species of bacteria—a whole ecosystem—on a clump of pumice the size of a human head.

Above opposite: Staghorn corals reproduce sexually and asexually—if a branch breaks off, it sometimes reattaches itself to the substrate and forms a new colony.

Above left and right: Healthy coral colonies on the Reef.

Clams breed by releasing their eggs and sperm in several convulsive closures, squirting the gametes up into the water column to speed their rise to the surface. Some of the stinging hydroids and soft corals release small medusae, which are like little sea jellies, of both sexes. These medusae release the eggs and sperm, which go through the same cycle as the hard corals.

Hydroids include the stinging corals and the stinging ferns. They have evolved a different process of reproduction—instead of the sea jelly, its cousin, being a general living form, it is only released as a small free-swimming individual for breeding.

This mass spawning can last for three or four hours, and by dawn visibility in the water may drop from 30 m (33 yd) to only 10 m (11 yd). The sea is covered with a pink–yellow slick of animal gametes or, perhaps by now, planulae larvae (see opposite). The slick, known as coral spawn, is often confused with blooms of the cyanobacteria, *Trichodesmium*, which result in a green or yellow to white slick with an unpleasant, pungent smell.

Divers call the water 'gamete soup' due to the loss of visibility and a fishy smell that clings to them as they leave the water.

Up on the reef tops, the spawning event has not affected the emergence of the asses's ear shell, octopi, eels and other night-time feeders that cruise the reef as they hunt.

As dawn breaks on a new day, the seabirds and pigeons are already heading for their foraging grounds while the fish and other species that had been sleeping in crevices, cocoons or sandy hideouts begin to emerge. The reef seems 'spent'—the fish have obviously gorged too much and the corals will need some time to recover, but for other species who neither spawn, nor feed on spawn, it is life as usual.

Warmer water temperatures

Once it has settled onto a surface, the small new coral colony is still vulnerable. Warm, still and humid summer days create the ideal conditions for the formation of a cyclone. As the warm, still waters heat the air, it begins to rise faster and faster, drawing in air from all around it. If that air is equally hot or hotter, a cyclone can develop.

These massive storms, called cyclones in the southern hemisphere (where they travel in a clockwise direction) but are known as hurricanes or typhoons in the northern hemisphere (where they travel anti-clockwise), can reach speeds of more than 250 km (155 mi) per hour. Which can cause storm surges and raise the sea level as much as 7 m (23 ft) in coastal areas, less offshore, as the updraft lifts the sea with it. When the sometimes massive waves formed in these storms hit a reef, they tear off old coral heads the size of a car and roll them through coral communities like a bulldozer.

After cyclones, these bare reef surfaces attract the growth of small algae, which form chains of threads or filaments containing a toxic substance called ciguatoxin. As small fish graze on the algae, they are eaten by bigger fish, so ciguatera gradually accumulates to the point where it can poison any humans who eat the top predator fish. These bare reef surfaces can also be ideal for the settlement of new coral larvae, so a reef wiped out by a cyclone or eaten by crown-of-thorns sea stars can often look 'perfect' as soon as ten years later.

There is another effect of higher than normal water temperatures. The polyps may be stressed by the zooxanthellae producing too much oxygen in

Previous spread left: A sea cucumber releases its egg bundles and smoke-like sperm.

Previous spread right: *Acropora millepora* coral release their egg and sperm bundles at the same time. The coral mass spawning event occurs in November each year, while crown-of-thorns sea stars spawn annually between December and April.

Above left: This satellite image shows Tropical Cyclone Yasi approaching Queensland on 2 February 2011. The Category 5 cyclone destroyed coral reefs more than 500 km (310 mi) from the storm front.

Above right: On 21 March 2010, yachts litter the shoreline after being washed ashore by Cyclone Ului at Shute Harbour, near Airlie Beach on the Queensland coast.

Opposite: Some specimens of bleached coral skeletons, from top to bottom: mushroom, needle and *Acropora*.

Left: After laying a clutch of up to 100 eggs, the green sea turtle makes the arduous journey from her nest back to the sea.

their tissues. To protect themselves, the polyps expel the algae, which turns the coral the most beautiful pastel shades of green, pink and blue and, finally, white. If you examine the white colonies, you'll see that the animal tissue is totally transparent, making the skeleton show pure white through the normally brown tissue. This coral bleaching process is becoming more common as climate change and other factors stress the reefs. The corals may recover fully but, if they die, they may become encrusted with algae or become the settlement site for the next spawning event.

A female green sea turtle can take several hours to find a suitable nesting place, a process made more difficult by the huge numbers of turtles who may converge on the same island.

Turtles and seabirds

On offshore islands thousands of seabirds may be nesting, producing masses of guano (faeces), once an important resource for guano miners (see page 206). Each day the adults roam far out to sea, returning at dusk or after dark to feed their chicks. But sometimes nesting turtles, coming ashore to lay, can have a devastating effect on the bird colony. These turtles, more than thirty years old, return to the beach where they hatched. As they lumber around the edge of the island, looking for the right spot to lay, it is common for them to destroy birds' nests and eggs and, in some cases, dig up the eggs laid by other turtles. On some sand cays in the north, nesting Torresian imperial pigeons bring seeds in their droppings, creating mini-rainforest habitats.

Right: During the annual breeding season, a pair of green sea turtles mate, attended by a secondary male. It has been known for up to six turtles to become involved. The green sea turtle, an endangered species, faces many dangers including fishing nets, pollution and loss of habitat. Humans in some countries also hunt turtle eggs and adults for food.

Future prospects

As the oceans become warmer and more acidic, overfishing disrupts food chains and coastal runoffs and high-speed boats carrying tourists upset their biochemistry, it becomes harder for reef animals and plants to survive.

If you're lucky enough to experience a whole twenty-four hour period on a reef—be it under water, walking the reefs or snorkelling—your life will be changed forever, especially if you're patient and pick out only a few animals to watch. As you discover more and your connection to the reef deepens, you'll understand why these ecosystems are so special and need our greatest efforts to ensure their survival.

4

MEETING THE PLANTS AND ANIMALS

In this fascinating underwater world, plants and animals have evolved ingenious ways to avoid predators. Before it settles down to rest for the night, the parrotfish exudes a layer of mucus, which it blows up around its body until the membrane forms a 'sleeping bag' that will prevent the fish's smell being detected by predators. The white-tip reef shark, however, can detect the movement of its muscles as it breathes.

A spectacular range of life forms

The greatest reef biodiversity on Earth can be found in the Coral Triangle, which is centred on the Celebes Sea north of Indonesia, despite the fact that this so-called 'Amazon of the seas' has been subjected to various destructive human activities, including land-clearing, explosive fishing (where schools of fish are blasted with explosives to make collection easier), poison fishing, limestone mining and general overuse.

To the average person a healthy reef will seem extraordinary even though it may be very low in species diversity. Henderson Atoll in the eastern Pitcairn Group, for example, is a spectacular diving site but it only has a tenth of the number of species on the Great Barrier Reef. It is the enormous number of habitats provided by coral reefs such as the Great Barrier Reef and also those that impact on them that result in such a high degree of biodiversity. To date only the larger species groups—such as echinoderms (sea stars), corals, fish and molluscs—have been well-studied.

In this chapter we will take a look at the simplest plants and animals to be found on the Great Barrier Reef, starting with microscopic life forms, then continue up the evolutionary tree to the more complex species, ending with mammals, such as whales, dolphins and dugongs.

Opposite: A selection of microscopic plankton species, which range in size from a fraction of a millimetre to several centimetres. There is a vast array of microscopic life in Great Barrier Reef waters.

The microscopic world

Cyanobacteria and microscopic blue–green algae are extremely important in all marine systems. They can fix nitrogen from the atmosphere or water and, via photosynthesis, add it to the essential nutrients they need. They are found as massive blooms floating in Reef waters, in algal mats on the sea or lagoon floors, on bare rocky surfaces, and in sponges (which they supply with essential nutrients) and many other organisms. Some species are found inside the abandoned coral skeleton, under the living tissues, where they act as bio-eroders, gradually destroying the structure.

Plants and animals of the Reef ecosystem

For some of these plants and animals, the number of species recorded is provided, but for others the most up-to-date estimate is given. Note that this table does not include Torres Strait.

Plants and animals	No. of species recorded
Bony fish	1625
Crocodiles	1
Crustaceans	About 1300
Dugongs	1
Echinoderms	630
Hard corals	411
Mangroves	39
Marine macroalgae	630
Marine turtles	6
Molluscs	Up to 3000
Sea snakes	14 breeding species
Seabirds	22 nesting species
Seagrass	15
Sharks and rays	134
Soft corals and sea pens	At least 150
Sponges	At least 3000
Whales and dolphins	More than 30
Worms	At least 500

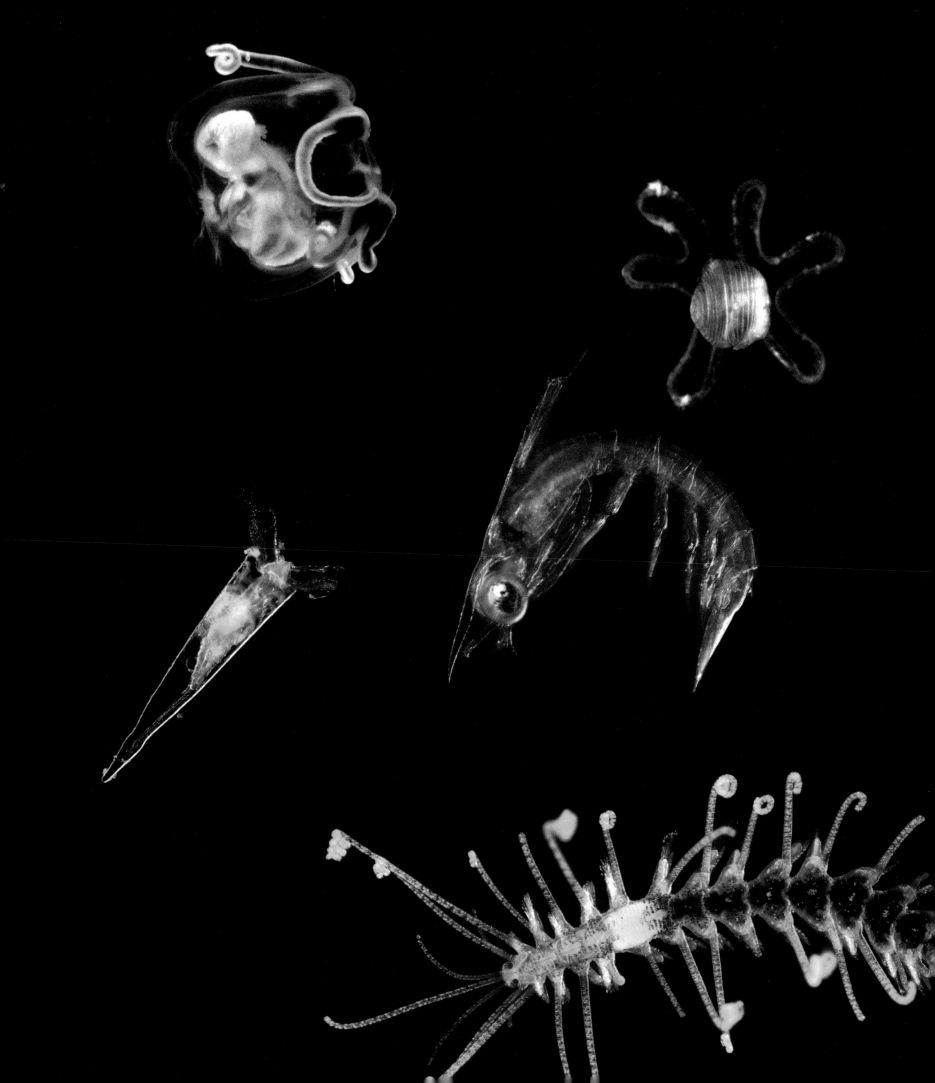

Algae

There are three main types of algae—red, green and brown. They have no flowers, leaves or roots but they convert sunlight, carbon dioxide and other nutrients into energy for growth. There is almost every size and shape of algae imaginable, including the giant kelps, which are found in very cold water environs, and also the sargassums, found throughout the world.

A major food source for many grazing species, algae are found in every habitat on the Great Barrier Reef. The crustose or coralline forms are also very important in the formation of reefs, as they protect the reef fronts from the enormous forces of waves and also cement together old skeletons, shells and rubble to form the matrix of a reef.

There are more than 630 known species of macroalgae found on the Great Barrier Reef, but this is only a preliminary list.

①② *Trichodesmium* blooms

Often confused with 'coral spawn' or even oil slicks, *Trichodesmium* blooms contribute a massive amount of biomass to the Great Barrier Reef system. Much of it could be caused by nutrients, such as fertilisers, in runoffs from coastal areas.

③④ *Zooxanthellae*

These small single-celled algae, which live in the coral polyps, are essential for the growth of reef-building hard corals. They absorb some of the coral's waste and some carbon dioxide from the water, in return producing oxygen and the raw products for corals to make sugars and proteins—true symbiosis, or living together for the common good (see also page 71). A byproduct of this process is calcium carbonate, which the polyp dumps at its base, forming a skeleton that is unique to each species.

① *Noctiluca scintillans*

These small algae, also known as sea sparkles, are one of the many plankters that have the capacity to create their own light. This bioluminescence—similar to lightsticks—can be seen in the wake of ships, on divers in the water and even in sea-water toilets on large ships.

② **Diatoms**

This group of usually single-celled microalgae have the most intriguing shapes. Encased in a skin of silica, diatoms are primary producers at the bottom of the food chain. When they die, they sink to the abyssal depths, creating a soft mud-like ooze that, when the sea floor is uplifted and mined, becomes the source of diatomaceous earths, so important in water filters and other manufactured products.

③ **Crustose or coralline algae**

These not only form the flat 'paint' algae we see on wave-battered reef fronts but also surround an old piece of coral rolled around on the reef top, forming what is known as an algalith, which is alive on all sides with coralline algae.

④ *Halimeda*

Halimeda is very special as it supplies an enormous amount of calcium carbonate to the reef system when it dies, after a life span of a few months to a year. The disc-shaped thalli—a thallus is an algal body—then turn white and become part of the sandy reef floor. Their surfaces are also often richly coated with diatoms and many other minute plant and animal species. In areas of the Reef north of Lizard Island there are massive living dunes of *Halimeda* and some associated species of algae (see also page 45).

⑤ **Filamentous algae**

Common on almost any newly exposed reef surface, filamentous algae can sometimes be seen as fixed healthy clumps on the reef top and elsewhere. They often host a green-coloured crab, which lives commensally in the algae.

Flowering plants

This section does not include species found on the mainland or on mainland islands.

Mangroves

Mangroves have been discussed in the chapter on habitats (see page 34). These sources of nutrients are also important to the reef system as toxin-filters, mud stabilisers and nurseries.

① Grey mangrove

The grey mangrove (*Avicennia*) creates beautiful glades in the mid-intertidal areas. Their pencil-thin aerial roots project about 10–20 cm (4–8 in) above the mud, allowing the trees to 'breathe'. These trees are found between a fringing reef and an island.

② Stilt-root mangrove

The red wood gives the red mangrove (*Rhizophora*) its name. It has distinctive stilt roots that help it to 'breathe'.

Seagrasses

Seagrasses, which flower once a year, can pop up here and there on intertidal mud- or sand flats, forming almost impenetrable crops or meadows up to 50 cm (20 in) deep. In Bathurst Bay in Northern Queensland, dugongs thrive on such rich pickings.

① *Halophila spinulosa*

There are about a dozen species of *Halophila*, and they range from strap- or ribbon-like forms through to thick, fleshy fern-like forms like this one.

② *Cymodocea serrulata*

There are several species and subspecies of this seagrass—often known as tape or ribbon weed—common around Australia. Each blade provides a perfect surface for many smaller plants and animals to live and feed on.

Beach strandline plants

Essential for stabilising cays and beaches, these are seen on the islands of the Great Barrier Reef and almost all the way around the coast of Australia.

③ **Goat's foot convolvulus**

This spreading dune vine bears broad leaves, which resemble a goat's footprints, and beautiful pink flowers like trumpets—hence its other common name, beach morning glory. Roots appear at each branching node. As its seeds aren't affected by seawater, the vine is found around the world on tropical to subtropical coastlines.

④ **Beach spinifex**

A tough tussocky grass that can grow up to 1 m (3 ft) high, beach spinifex sends tendrils across the dunes, thus helping to stabilise them. There are several similar species of grasses and sedges that also bond the sand.

⑤ Horsetail she-oaks

Inside the strandline colonisers, the sand becomes stable enough for the establishment and growth of the horsetail she-oaks. These trees are highly atmospheric plants, as they constantly whisper in the breeze. Several species of birds nest in them, and many of these trees are used for roosting. On Heron Island the tides draining out of the channel resulted in the erosion of almost 30 m (33 yd) of beach right around the island, the demise of old she-oaks and the exposure of the beachrock ridges. These exposed ridges reveal older fossilised beach lines that are less than 5000 years old.

⑥ Octopus bush

So named because their fruiting bunches look like the underside of an octopus' tentacle, these important strandline stabilisers also provide nest sites for a variety of birds.

① *Pisonia*

Although pisonia forests, which provide a full canopy with very little understorey, are common on the coral cays of the southern Great Barrier Reef, they are not found anywhere else in Australia. They are used by thousands of nesting black noddy terns (see page 132), which suffer enormous losses when storms wreck the nests or blow over the trees. After such destruction the trees send up vertical 'limbs' from the horizontal stems, establishing new plants. The areas between the trees are not only rich in litter but also home to burrowing wedge-tailed shearwaters and the scuttling banded land rails.

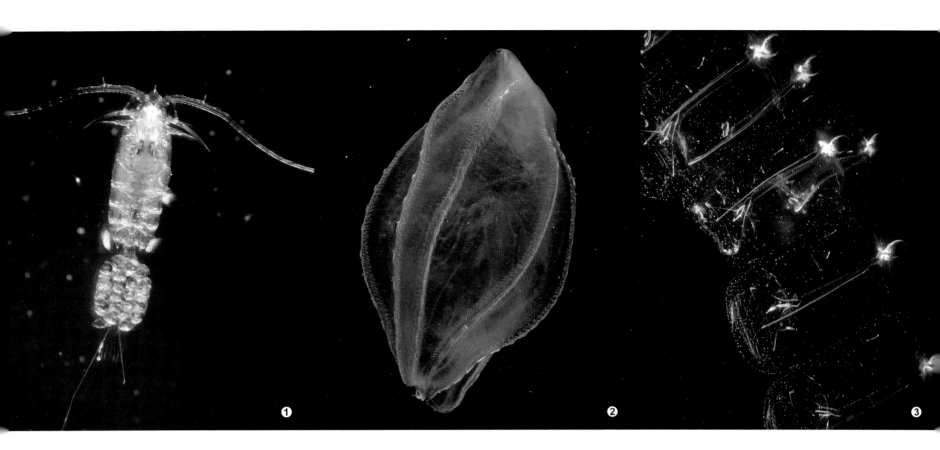

① ② ③

Invertebrate animals

These animals have no backbones, and are either fully soft or use a variety of other methods to maintain their rigidity.

Planktonic animals

Ranging in size from microns to metres across, these free-floating animals present an enormous challenge to the researcher, as some preserve well when they are captured while others shatter completely, or are eaten by other animals in the samples before they can be preserved. Planktonic animals use oil, gas, body extensions and cilia (little hairs) to help them stay in the water depth of their choice, which changes according to whether it is day or night.

① Copepods

The name of these animals means 'oar-feet', and they can be found in almost any water mass or damp area. They eat diatoms (see page 95) and are in turn eaten by plankton-eating fish, baleen whales and birds. Both their faeces and their dead bodies are a constant source of food for the ooze dwellers on the sea floor.

② Ctenophores

Sea gooseberries, sea walnuts, comb jellies and other names are applied to this diverse group of animals, which are best seen underwater, as they usually do not survive being captured. Rows of cilia running down their sides enable them to move, and some store unfired stinging cells from their prey, the 'stinger' jellies. They can grow up to 15 cm (6 in) long.

③ Salps

These fascinating barrel-shaped animals, a form of sea squirt, can usually be found in long linear colonies that break up easily. Their larvae have a basic notochord, like a soft backbone, making them early relatives of humans in the evolutionary tree. When there are massive plant plankton blooms, the salps bud rapidly, almost flooding the ocean. Their dead bodies and faeces also add to the oozes on the oceanic sea floor.

Non-planktonic animals

These fix themselves to other animals or plants, or to the sea floor.

Sponges

The most primitive of all the multicellular animals, sponges have been on Earth for 750 million years or more. They created reefs in times past, and can be found in most reef habitats, where they pull water through their bodies, absorbing oxygen and nutrients. Sponges outnumber the species of hard and soft corals combined. They play many roles, from supplying a primary industry and filtering waste products to accumulating toxins and recycling calcium carbonate back into the reef system.

Some 400 species of sponge on the Reef have been described, but there are at least 2500 more. Reproducing either sexually or by asexual budding, sponges exhibit enormous variations and occur in all habitats. The complexity of chemicals they contain and use has made them the focus of much pharmaceutical research.

① Encrusting sponges

If you look carefully at the surface of an encrusting sponge, you will see many small holes (inhalant siphons) and a few larger ones (exhalant siphons). Each sponge is a colony of specialised individual cells—for breeding, feeding, pumping and holding onto the bottom. These sponges collect toxins from captured animals, then use them to kill off any animal that tries to grow too close to them or eat them. Encrusting sponges vary greatly in colour and can be found in every reef habitat. Some are ferocious colonisers, able to kill living coral colonies and grow over the top of them, especially when they are stressed.

② Cup sponges

Some smashed up cup sponges will reassemble themselves back into their colony if they are left in good water. To see how much water cup sponges can pump through their bodies each day, sprinkle a little fine sediment above one. You will see the water flow immediately speed up.

Cnidarians

Cnidarians—including sea jellies, anemones, sea whips, zooanthids, corallimorpharians, stinging hydroids, hard corals and soft corals—comprise an enormous group of animals that possess specially modified cells called nematocysts, or stinging cells. Some well-known species are the free-swimming sea jellies, such as the box jellyfish, irukandji (of which there are at least ten species), jimble, blue-bottle, sea walnut and sea gooseberry.

③ Box jellyfish
Easily identified by its cubed body shape, the box jellyfish or sea wasp can range in size from 1 cm (½ in) to 30 cm (1 ft) across. Almost all species have the capacity to kill humans— each of their tentacles may contain almost a million stinging cells.

④ Irukandji
At only 1 cm (½ in) across, the irukandji is an extremely venomous cuboid jelly, which can be found throughout the world's oceans.

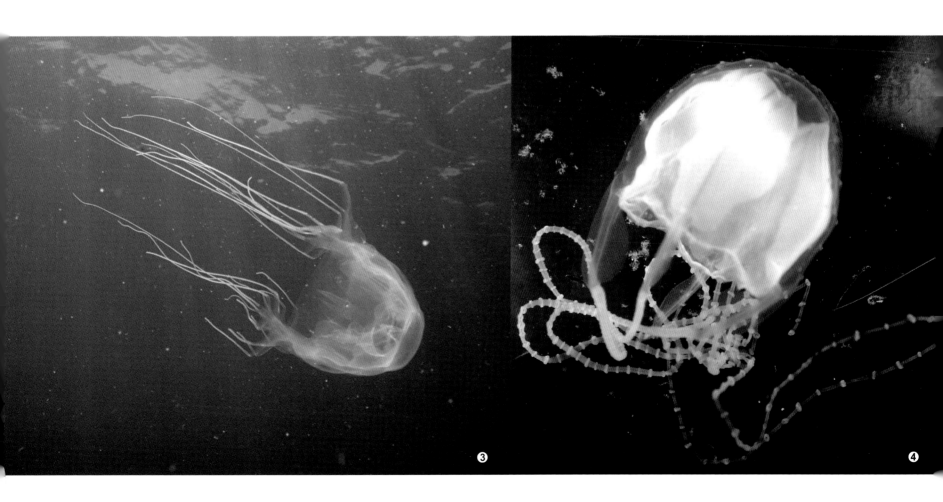

③ ④

Actiniarians

The actinarians include anemones and their five 'cousins'. They have no hard skeleton and do not contribute to reef-building. Like the hard and soft corals, they have a long polyp stage and a short, sexually produced larval stage. Some, like the antipatharians (see page 106), produce a hard skeleton of a protein-like material. These are often known as black corals, once prized as jewellery but now protected under the Convention on International Trade in Endangered Species.

①②③ *Anemones*

Named after the *Anemone* garden flower, anemones come in a huge variety of forms, ranging in size from 2 cm (¾ in) to 2 m (6½ ft) across. They have an adhesive foot with a column-shaped gut. Once the anemone captures its prey, it uses a tentacle to deliver it to its mouth. The clownfish keep their tentacles clean and capture extra prey (see also page 71). In exchange, the fish's mucous coat protects it from the anemone stings, making it possible to hide in the anemone and avoid predators.

① Zooanthids

These are much more common in other environments than all their coral cousins. They form colonies of single polyps side by side or on a mat made up of sediments. The colours each colony exhibits vary a great deal.

② Corallimorpharia

Another cousin of the anemones, these tropical animals feature a wide disc—rather than tentacles—around the mouth, and a smaller gut and base. They usually occur in clusters, and can badly sting an unprotected diver.

③ Antipatharia

The best known of these is the black coral. They have a similar body structure to their actinarian cousins (see page 105), but form a horny skeleton covered by the individual polyps.

Hard corals

Hexacorrallia, or hard corals, which all feature a hexagonal body shape, include the actinarians or non-reef-building groups and also the scleractinians or reef-building hard corals. They all lay down a calcium carbonate skeleton that is external to the animal. These hard corals are the true reef-building corals. They reproduce primarily sexually in what has become well-known as the 'upside down snowstorm' when the gametes are released (see page 77).

It is the zooxanthellae, the small single-celled algae living symbiotically in the coral tissue (see page 59) that allow the hard corals to produce their skeletal material.

④ Pocilloporidae

This brown-stem knobby coral is often targeted by the acquariam and commercial trade and sold in shops as ornaments.

⑤ Acroporidae

Probably one of the most spectacular and best-known of the reef-building corals, staghorn coral can grow up to 10 cm (4 in) per year. Some are highly robust and lie almost flat on the reef crest, while other species grow 5 m (16 ft) high and as thin as a finger in calm lagoons.

⑥ Poritidae

Best known as kidney coral, the shape formed by the small colonies of polyp animals, poritidae grow up to 10 m (33 ft) across. Some may be as much as several thousand years old.

① *Goniopora*

Best known as the 'daytime' coral, because their tentacles feed day and night, goniopora have skeletons that are usually lighter than those species with a higher zooxanthellae count. They also 'farm' the zooxanthellae during the day, as do other hard reef-building corals (see page 59).

② **Fungiidae**

Mushroom corals look like beautiful copies of the underside of a mushroom, or are twisted and gnarled, long and oblong in shape. Most are free-living solitary animals. Each begins life as a small animal attached to a stalk. When it reaches about 5 cm (2 in) across, the stem is weakened by its burrowing resident worms, so the animal breaks off and lives free. The mushroom coral is very silt-resistant, and can pump up its tissue until it lifts the heavy skeleton out of the mud.

③ **Mussidae**

This widespread family of usually spiky, sinuous, thick, fleshy and colourful polyps includes some of the biggest colonial polyps. During the annual spawning event, these hermaphrodites release both eggs and sperm into the water.

④ **Faviidae**

Faviidae tend to form massive ball-shaped colonies. This very important coral group includes numerous species that also have a similar hermaphroditic reproductive cycle. Some bud inside the polyp as the coral grows, while others bud outside the parent polyp. Look at the photograph and see if you can work out which is which.

⑤ *Tubastrea*

Tubastrea are spectacular yellow, red and green corals that form hard single polyp tubes, generally in clusters. They do not form reefs, as they have no symbiotic zooxanthellae in their tissues and the colour comes from the animal itself (see page 59). One particular species can be seen in deeper waters, competing with hard corals, but most restrict themselves to cave tops and under overhangs.

⑥ **Stylaster**

Their colonies of usually delicate pink, tree-like corals—normally found in protected microhabitats such as under overhangs and in caves—do not contribute to reef growth. The living animals can be seen in the grooves that run along the edges of the branches.

⑦ **Millepora**

Depending on their reef habitat, stinging or fire corals form massive, branching or carpeting hard colonies. Each has two types of holes on its surface—a larger 'mouth' surrounded by smaller 'hair' holes; the stinging cells are within the hairs. The sting is a little stronger than nettles but very itchy, and scratching the affected skin often leads to infections.

Soft corals

Soft corals (Octocorallia) are non-reef-building animals that live fixed to the bottom of the sea floor. They have eight tentacles, unlike their cousins, the hard corals, which have six, or multiples of six (see page 107). Some produce calcareous spicules that aid their support, and some fuse them into a base that endures, forming soft reef rock.

① *Sarcophyton*

The soft corals in this very robust group have many common names, such as leathery coral and toadstool coral. They can withstand areas of high siltation due to an ability to shed a waxy layer with the silt. Some species lay down a skeleton of spicules, which can contribute to reef growth. These soft corals also house zooxanthellae, and will bleach when the water temperature is high (see page 82). In this image you can see the sarcophyton spawning.

② Gorgonian corals

Fan corals—sea-whips, fans, candelabra, sheet and web-fan shapes—can be found on most coral reefs. Their polyps emerge from their horny skeleton and feed on plankton at night. Some whips can reach up to 5 m (16 ft) in length, while fans can grow up to several metres across.

③ *Dendronephthya*

Spiky soft corals are some of the Reef's beauties. Ranging in colour from bright reds, yellows and orange to pink and purple, they can be found from the shallows to very deep waters, where the colonies can grow up to 2 m (6½ ft) in height. They maintain their shape by keeping themselves pumped full of water but, when exposed on a reef top at low tide, they become limp and fall over.

Worms

There is a stunning diversity of worm shapes, sizes, life cycles, habits and places where they are found on all reefs: segmented worms, or those with long, flat ribbon-like forms; some that look like peanuts until they extrude their probosces, which may be twice as long as their bodies; and split ribbon or spoon worms, which put out feeding tentacles up to 1 m (3 ft) from their bodies, then use tiny hairs called cilia to carry food back down the ribbons to their mouths. There are also hair worms, parasitic tapeworms, flukes and free-living flatworms.

① Polychaetes

Segmented bristle worms, which come in a huge variety of shapes and sizes, are found in a range of locations. If you pick them up, fire worms will break off their spikes, which will burn your skin. Some beach species can be 2 m (6½ ft) long but others just a few centimetres. Some, like the Christmas-tree worms pictured, live embedded in coral skeletons, withdrawing their feeding and breathing tentacles whenever they are threatened.

② Flatworms

Flatworms can be quickly distinguished from nudibranch molluscs, with which they are often confused, by their thin body layer, two tentacles and the fact that they have no other projecting parts. They will often be found living on sea cucumbers in a symbiotic relationship (see page 71), or free-living on the substrate.

③ Ribbon worms

You will rarely see ribbon worms—long, sinuous, sticky, unsegmented worms—unless you turn over boulders or catch one out and about at night. Usually brightly coloured, they can range from a few millimetres to 1 m (3 ft) in length.

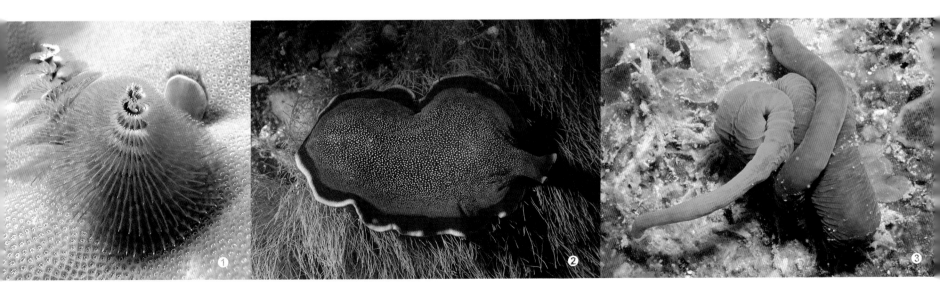

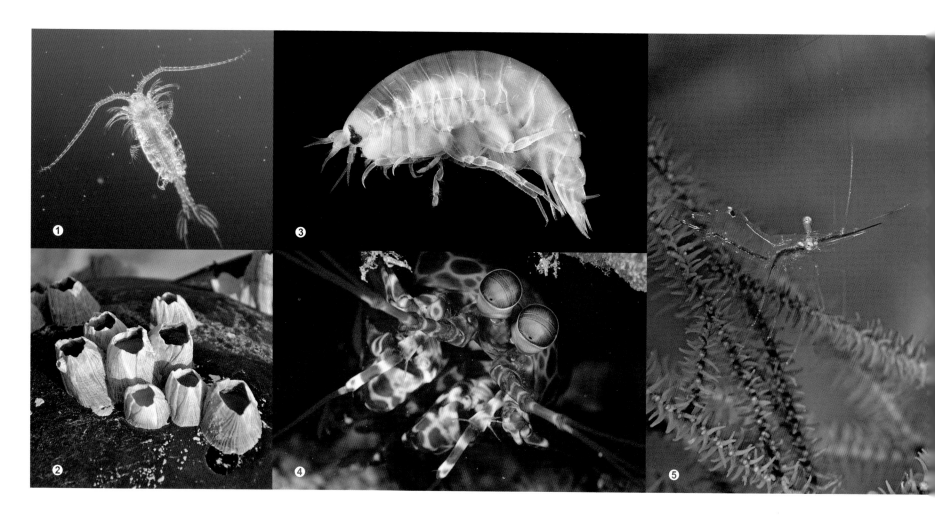

Crustaceans

Marine arthropods, or crustaceans, which feature a chitinous (fingernail-like material) exoskeleton (external skeleton), are related to the insects on land and are just about as diverse. Found in the shallowest of reef waters and also down in the abyssal depths, crustaceans include minute plank-tonic forms, crabs, barnacles, prawns (shrimp) and prawn-killers as well as lobsters and crayfish.

① Copepods

Copepods (oar-feet) can be seen in a vast array of shapes. Most are free-living in fresh and salt water, with many species being parasitic. They are abundant on the Great Barrier Reef—among the sand grains on the beaches and sea floor; in the plankton, where they are ferocious predators but also become prey to many larger animals; and in every reef habitat. The best-known are those that live with amphipods (beach hoppers) among the rotting vegetation on the beach strandline, where wading birds feast on them.

② Barnacles

Essentially crabs with their backs glued to the rocks and legs kicking in the air, barnacles are highly modified filter feeders. As the waters rise over them, they start kicking their legs in the water to capture prey. They are found on most intertidal surfaces and on floating objects such as buoys, logs and other flotsam and jetsam.

③ Amphipoda

Usually amphipoda are flattened on each side. Pick up any piece of beach litter and you will see sand hoppers—the best-known of all amphipods—hop away, then quickly bury themselves in the sand. They may be grazers, parasites, carnivores or detriti-vores—that is, they feed on decomposing plant and animal parts. Found in almost every habitat, most amphipods are yet to be named.

④ Stomatopods

Mantis shrimp are common on the Great Barrier Reef but are usually found only in shallow waters. The reef-top forms are a vivid green while their cousins, who burrow into the sand floors of the shallow lagoons, are usually white to transparent. They are extremely aggressive predators—some have club-like forelegs they use to bludgeon their prey while others have spear-like forelegs they use to spear their victims (see also page 152).

⑤ Prawns (shrimp)

Prawns (shrimp) are caught by fishing trawlers and eaten as seafood. An enormous number of shrimp, not of commercial interest, can be found in every Great Barrier Reef underwater habitat. It is common to see swarms of juveniles in habitats such as mangroves, seagrasses, *Halimeda* meadows and among other algae. In the right conditions they will also swarm as adults and juveniles in estuaries.

⑥ Crayfish

Closely related to lobsters and also to Moreton Bay or Balmain bugs, crayfish forage at night. They have five pairs of legs, but the front legs have powerful pincers used for capturing and grasping food. Their forward-pointing spines allow them to lock themselves into the overhangs, where they spend the day.

⑦ Hermit crabs

Hermit crabs, which can be up to 30 cm (1 ft) long, have a specially adapted body shape that allows them to slide into a dead mollusc shell to protect their tender abdomens. Both marine and land forms can be found, and you can identify some species by checking which claw is larger—the left (the left-handed hermit crab) or the right (the right-handed hermit crab).

⑧ Crabs

There are about 500 species of true crabs to be found in every habitat on the Great Barrier Reef, even on floating pumice rafts or logs. At night beach-goers will see—but probably not be able to catch—ghost crabs, while reef-walkers will be able to see a great variety of other species, ranging from transparent through all colours to blacks and browns.

Molluscs

In Reef waters there are at least 3000 known species of molluscs or seashells, but many more are to yet to be described. Most are free-living, feeding by grazing or filtering, while others are very destructive, burrowing into coral skeletons. A few are parasitic. The body shapes and sizes vary a great deal. They are also very important in both the bio-erosion of the reef and the supply of dead shell material for reef growth. Some, such as the giant clam and its near relatives, also act as 'farmers' with the zooxanthellae in their tissues (see page 59).

About 2500 of these species are single-shelled gastropods. Of the molluscan group on the Reef, these are the most diverse and numerous. They include sea snails and limpets (shelled), and also sea hares and nudibranchs—these have no shells or perhaps a thin internal remnant of one. They have a distinct head and a muscular foot, which they use to glide over the substrate, hence the name gastropods, or 'stomach-feet', as they seem to move along on their stomachs. Many species with a shell also have an operculum (little lid), which the animal uses to close over the opening when it withdraws into its shell.

① Gastropods

Baler shells are bizarre, as the animals are far too big for their shells. As these predators cruise the reef for food, they use their extended probosces to sniff the waters like an elephant's trunk.

② Sea hares

Superbly camouflaged, sea hares glide across the reef flat, feeding on algae. When they are disturbed, they release purple ink, which was used in ancient times to dye Roman emperors' robes. Their name derives from the club-shaped rhinophores—reminiscent of a hare's ears—they use for smell. Shown here is a mating pair. The two large flaps of tissue on the animals' backs hide the gills.

③ Chitons

Chain-of-mail shell—whose shells have been reduced to small plates along their backs—is a great name for these grazers, which live on rocks and other hard surfaces in intertidal zones, moving back to exactly the same location at high tide; one theory is that they leave behind a chemical trail. They come out to graze on algae and other foods at low tide, when the weather is cooler or darkness descends.

④ **Nudibranch**

Literally 'naked gills'—in most shells the gills are hidden inside the shell—the vibrantly coloured nudibranch moves around the reef top. Some species feed on fire coral or stinging hydroids, then transfer the stinging cells to the waving flaps of tissue on their backs to ward off predators. Their often brilliant colours also warn predators they may not be so tasty.

① **Giant clams**

If you'd like to experience a breathtaking sight, float over a multicoloured giant clam with its mantle—the outer body wall and the fins—wide open, 'farming' its zooxanthellae (see page 59). As your shadow hits the clam, it will convulsively close. Look deep into the clam and you will be able to see its gills and other internal organs, which are important in the filtering/feeding process at night. Shown here is a burrowing clam (see also page 65), which has burrowed into a coral.

② **Cephalopods**

Squid, cuttlefish and octopus all belong to a group of molluscs called cephalopods, meaning 'head-feet'. All have eight tentacles or arms—except for squid, which have ten, with two much longer tentacles used for snapping up prey at a distance—and an incredible ability to change colours according to their background. When mating, they send superb flashes and pulses of colour along their bodies.

① Lace corals

Also known as bryozoans, lace corals secrete their own little chambers in which to live. In colder waters they are known to form massive underwater ridges and small reefs. They are one of the least known groups worldwide, with many species still to be identified. Other growth forms are bushy and mat-like. Each colony is made up of the most complex combination of 'animals' seen in the animal kingdom. Some are for feeding, some for holding on, while others are for breeding, food transport, spines, space-fillers, and more. Found only under overhangs or in similar protected sites, these superb pastel-coloured lace corals are very fragile.

Echinoderms

We know these spectacular and colourful spiny-skinned animals as feather stars, sea stars, brittle-stars, sea urchins, sand dollars and sea cucumbers. Found in almost every Great Barrier Reef habitat, these fascinating creatures are usually far more widespread than many other groups. Although there is little apparent similarity between the groups, they all have articulated spiny calcareous plates as an internal skeleton, move by using a highly sophisticated water hydraulic system and are based on pentaradial (five-fold) symmetry around a central region. As they have no 'head', they have an oral (mouth) and aboral (non-mouth) surface. All reproduce sexually, but most sea stars will regrow if cut into pieces, as long as a significant part of the central disk remains. Sea cucumbers can voluntarily split themselves into two halves and grow into two new animals.

❶ ❷

② Sea urchins

These small, spiny animals are based on the same five-fold symmetry as sea stars. If you find their egg-shaped or globular tests (shells)—beautiful constructions of interconnecting calcium carbonate plates—on the beach, you will see the sockets for the base of their spines, which will turn to face a predator. Some have toxic pedicellarie (claw-shaped extensions) between their spines.

③ Feather stars

Feather stars, which have a cluster of spines on their base to hold them to the substrate or soft coral fans, reach out into the current to capture food as it floats past. Many have commensal worms, shrimps and gobies living within their magnificently coloured, feathery masses. If displaced, some will swim by, waving their opposite arms up and down.

④ Sea stars

The best known echinoderms are the sea stars, which are also called starfish, although they are not fish. In this group you will find a huge range of sizes, colours, degrees of rigidity and thickness and preferred habitat. Some are carnivores—such as the coral-eating crown-of-thorns sea star, sponges, molluscs and even their cousins—but others are herbivores and detrital feeders.

⑤ Crown-of-thorns sea star

Covered in poisonous thorn-like spines, these echinoderms can invade reefs in plague proportions and eat all the live coral, but many experts believe these plagues occur only in reefs stressed by poor water quality. A reef totally stripped by sea stars may have a neighbouring reef with no crown-of-thorns sea stars at all. It may take at least ten years for the coral to look spectacular again, but many slower-growing species take much longer.

③

④

⑤

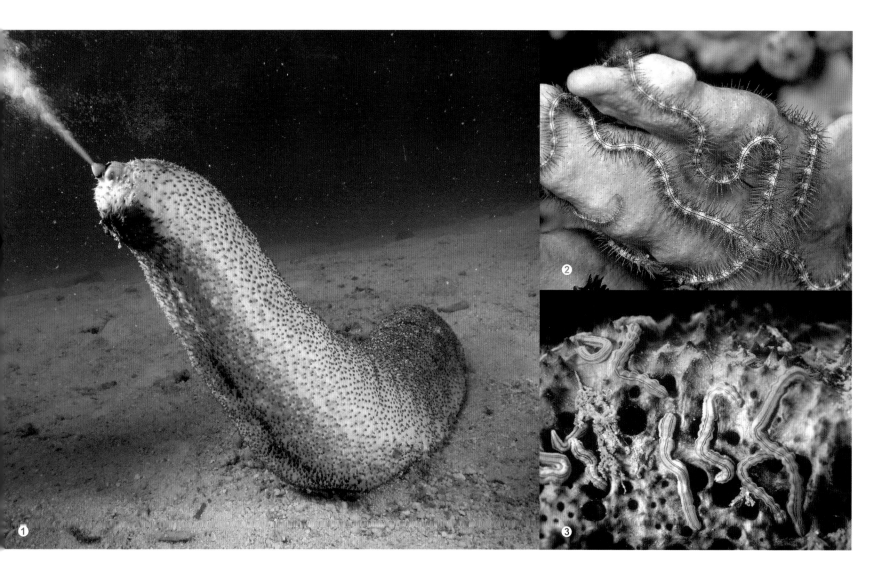

① Sea cucumbers

Once called beche-de-mer (from the French for 'sea spade'), sea cucumbers are affectionately known as the 'vacuum cleaners' of the sea. Their feathery tentacles are in constant motion, picking up a mixture of food and sand as they move through the Reef, leaving behind a mucous-covered rope of faeces. Several species live in a burrow in the sea floor, with their tentacles out feeding, often day and night. Many species have commensal shrimps or flatworms living on them; others have parasitic snails. Shown in the image above is a spawning male with the sperm spewing out from the genital pore on its 'head end' (see page 77).

② Brittle stars

Often known as snake or serpent stars, with tube feet that detect light, brittle stars can usually be detected when they extend their highly flexible arms from a reef-top crevice, but you won't see the whole animal unless you turn over a boulder, or disturb it in some other way. Even then they will quickly disappear into the nearest crevice.

③ Synaptids

The synaptid has thousands of tiny calcium carbonate spicules in its skin, some shaped like small, perfect anchors, giving the animal a sticky feeling. These needle-like thorns are generally used in species identification. Ranging in length from 2 cm (¾ in) to more than 2 m (6½ ft), this group occurs in most habitats, with the smaller ones on the reef top and the larger ones on muddy or sandy bottoms.

Tunicates or sea squirts

The free-swimming larvae of these sack-like creatures have a primitive backbone, which they lose once they cement themselves to a hard surface on the sea floor and develop into adults. Most of these plankton-feeders live in the mud or on the sandy sea floor, but many species can also be found in the plankton themselves. (Note the salps in the plankton section on page 101.) There are many forms living in many different habitats, with cunjevoi being the best known.

① Solitary sea squirts

The chemicals in sea squirts are of great interest to the pharmaceuticals industry as medicines. The bottom-dwelling forms may live as single animals or in colonies; they all display beautiful colours (except for the intertidal species, which tend to be covered in algae). Look carefully and you will always see a pair of siphons, allowing them to pump a huge amount of water through their bodies and thus capture food.

② Colonial sea squirts

It is common to see beautiful blue, yellow or orange mats of barrel-shaped colonial sea squirts. It is easy to confuse these mat-like forms with encrusting sponges (see page 102), until you note the pair of holes in the surface rather than the random holes seen in sponges.

Vertebrates

This group of higher order animals all have a back-bone as well as a well-developed head and brain.

Fish

On any reef, fish are the most predominant life form. You may see hundreds of species in a small area, often exhibiting bizarre behaviour. It is best to concentrate on one or two species, if you can, and learn from them. Remember, sharks have been in existence for at least 400 million years.

① White-tip reef sharks

The white-tip reef shark is one of the many shark species that can lie still and pump water through their gills, unlike other species that must extract oxygen from seawater as it flows over their gills. Growing to almost 2 m (6½ ft) long, this species is commonly found on most reef tops and drop-offs.

② Silver-tip sharks

The silver-tip is a strikingly beautiful shark, up to 3 m (10 ft) long, with brilliant white-edged fins and a superb, classic shark shape. Once it was common for divers to encounter these aggressive predators on the outer edge of the reef as they entered the water, but they are now a rarity.

③ Black-tip reef sharks

Often known as the black vee due to the dark V-shaped tips on its tail, the black-tip reef shark is another common species. If you dive below about 20 m (65½ ft), they'll stay away from you but continue to make curious passes.

④ Whale sharks

The world's biggest fish—spanning up to 15 m (49 ft) in length and weighing up to 40 tonnes (44 tons)—is the whale shark, a formidable-looking predator until you see this filter feeder's mouth, with its very tiny teeth and comb-like gills, which it uses to capture food. Whale shark congregation sites have become global tourist attractions, and there are at least three on the Great Barrier Reef, with the best-known one being in Wreck Bay in the Far Northern Region.

⑤ Manta rays

Another friendly filter-feeding giant of the ocean, these curious, completely harmless creatures will often swim close to divers, especially at night when their lights attract the plankton on which the ray feeds. The reef species can span 5 m (16 ft) across, while the oceanic species can reach 8 m (26 ft).

⑥ Cow-tailed rays

The cow-tailed ray is one of the species of ray that carries a toxin-laden barb in its tail. If you threaten one, or tread on it, the ray will flex its tail up and over, then down, stabbing you. It is usually harmless, unless it feels threatened.

⑦ Spotted moray eels

Their needle-sharp teeth give morays a ferocious appearance, especially as they must open and close their mouths as they breathe. Morays have been known to inflict severe wounds on humans, but only as a reaction to being speared, for example. The different species can be seen on reef tops in pools or down the reef slopes in most reef habitats.

① Squirrelfish

Night-feeding squirrelfish will almost always be found hovering in crevices, caves or under over hangs, waiting to move out to feed with the night shift, when their favourite prey, the crabs and prawns (shrimp), are also out and about. Divers on night dives may hear their clicking sounds.

② Seahorses

Seahorses and their elongated pipefish cousins can be found in seagrasses, algae beds and many reef habitats. They feed by plucking plankton from the water or from coral surfaces. In many species the male will carry the young in a special pouch on his abdomen. Some species are minute and beautifully camouflaged, matching the red sea fans on which they live.

③ Scorpionfish

This group includes lionfish and stonefish, all of which have a toxin-filled bulb at the base of each of their dorsal and pectoral spines. They lie in wait for their prey, then dash forward and gulp unsuspecting fish that come too close.

④ Potato cods

The younger individuals in this amazing group are females but after a few years they become male. Members of the cod family, including groupers, can reach 3 m (10 ft) long and weigh up to 400 kg (882 lb). Potato cods have never been known to be dangerous to humans, but they have taken dogs as they were swimming out to yachts in harbours.

⑤ Trevally

Often known as jacks, trevally are high-speed predators that are likely to appear out of the gloom and snap up small fish anywhere, any time. The giant trevally can grow to 1.7 m (5½ ft) long and weigh 75 kg (165 lb). The most spectacular is the blue-fin trevally, whose body has a delightful blue hue with iridescent-fringed fins.

⑥ Anthias

A joy to watch, and popular fish for aquariums, anthias or plankton pluckers are superbly coloured in pinks, yellows and oranges. Any food or larvae moving towards a reef must confront them—leaders in the wall of mouths waiting for their next meal. They dash out into the dangerous waters, away from the protection of the reef, and feed.

① **Sweetlips**

Also known as 'tricky snappers', sweetlips are found around shallow bommies and reef tops where they prey on other reef fish. Some species, called the red throat emperor, have a distinctive red mouth and throat as well as large eyes for feeding at night. Shown in the photograph above is a school of diagonally banded sweetlips.

② **Angelfish**

With their blue- and yellow-striped bodies, emperor angelfish are one of the most spectacular members of this group and also one of the hardest to see, as they hide from predators such as pilot whales and squid in cracks and crevasses. Most angelfish are territorial and feed on corals or the small animals living among them. Pictured are regal angelfish.

③ **Damselfish**

A large group found in a diverse range of habitats, displaying a range of behaviours and eating varied foods, damselfish can range from neon blues and yellows to the drabbest browns and greens to black. This group also includes the clownfish, which lives among anemones (see page 71). Some damselfish are so territorial that they will attack a human entering 'their' space. The females lay their eggs on a cleared space on the sea floor, where the male protects them.

④ Butterfly fish

With their diverse colours and patterns and their balletic dancing around the reef, butterfly fish are enthralling to watch. The majority live in the shallows, so they are easier to see as they feed on coral polyps, small crustaceans, algae and any other food that suits their small mouths.

⑤ Cleaner wrasse

Wrasse vary in size from 10 to 240 cm (4 to 7 ft) long and, in the case of the famed humphead or Maori wrasse, can weigh up to 190 kg (419 lb). The cleaner wrasse dances to attract fish to its cleaning station, where it picks off parasites and dead skin (see also page 62). Manta rays and other large fish will also attend the station and let the cleaner wrasse work inside their mouths and through their gills. Generally wrasse have two opposite pairs of teeth at the front of their mouths and smaller ones behind.

① **Parrotfish**

Parrotfish get their name from their fused teeth, giving their mouths the appearance of a parrot's beak. Until you see their mouths clearly, it is often hard to distinguish them from the wrasses. When the tide rises over the reef, you can see the parrot-fish tails poking out of the water as they graze on coral and algae.

② **Surgeonfish**

These aptly named fish feature retractable scalpel-like spines at the base of their tails. The blue-lined surgeonfish can turn vicious against other grazers when it protects its turf. Other species are more docile, but if you handle them incorrectly they will inflict a clean-cut wound.

③ Gobies

Gobies and their close relatives, the blennies and dartfish, are also among the most diverse groups of the Gobiidae family. They are usually small—4–12 cm (1–5 in) long—and occupy an enormous number of reef habitats. The goby lives with a shrimp, which keeps an antenna on it to ensure all is safe while the shrimp bulldozes out the burrow for them both (see also page 71).

④ Tuna

Like mackerel, marlin and sailfish—the speedsters of the ocean—tuna are top predators, smashing their way into bait balls of prey or snapping up any unwary fish. All tropical species will pass through parts of the Great Barrier Reef at various times of the year. A dog-tooth tuna is shown.

⑤ Flounder

Until it is disturbed, this small flounder is almost impossible to see on the muddy sea floor, then it moves away, flashing its spots to confuse predators. It feeds on smaller bottom-dwelling crabs, shrimp and the like.

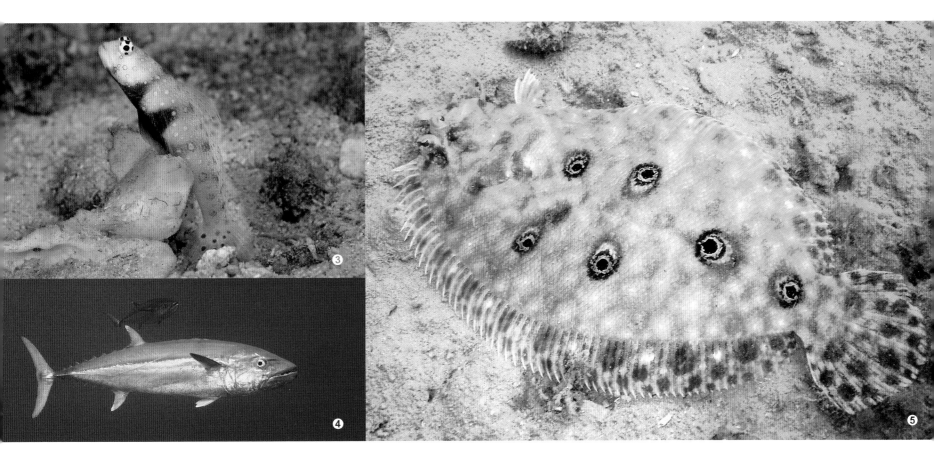

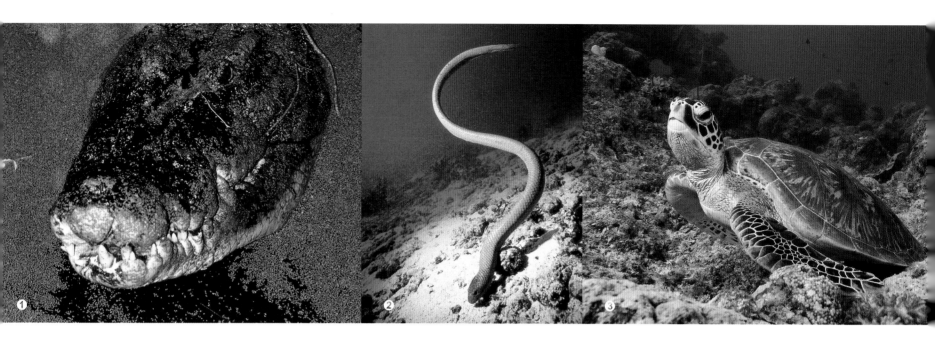

Reptiles

All reptiles breathe air, so the turtles, sea snakes and crocodiles in Reef waters can be seen when they regularly surface. These cold-blooded creatures tend to be found in tropical waters or warm current areas of higher latitudes. Most lay eggs on land, and a few give birth to live young. All have scales, or scutes, as skin.

① Estuarine crocodiles

Estuarine crocodiles remain within the rivers and estuaries of the coast, except when their populations become too large. Occasionally they have been found on islands of the northern Great Barrier Reef and, more rarely, thousands of kilometres out to sea.

② Sea snakes

Sea snakes are some of the world's most venomous species of snake but they rarely bite, unless they are severely provoked. They usually use their venom for capturing prey, usually fish, in the burrows and crevices of the Reef, especially at night.

③ Sea turtles

Sea turtles come ashore to lay their eggs on many islands and some mainland beaches of the Great Barrier Reef, and also further south. They take about thirty years to mature, and lay up to eight times in one year, then do not lay again for another three to five years. Their ancestors were living on Earth about 150 million years ago.

Seabirds

More than twenty species of seabird nest on the Great Barrier Reef, with some 175 species recorded in the Province. Many are residents, but others are in transit to, or from, breeding and feeding grounds. Many Reef islands are important sites for the survival of some species and important nesting areas for others, so it is vital to leave them undisturbed. Some islands are closed during bird-nesting season while others have restrictions in place. Silver gulls have learnt that whenever humans are present, nesting adults of other bird species will be frightened off their nests, so they immediately fly in to take the defenseless chicks or eggs.

① **Wedge-tailed shearwaters**

Generally referred to as 'mutton-birds', as they were once used as a food supply (some Aboriginal Australians still use them today for both cultural and food purposes), wedge-tailed shearwaters feed in the northern hemisphere over winter and arrive on the Reef on almost the same day every year to return to their burrows and raise their chicks.

Each female lays only a single egg per breeding season. When the chick is heavier than an adult bird and still downy, it is abandoned and left to grow out of its down into full plumage; it then follows its parents back to the northern hemisphere.

② **Brown boobies**

The name 'booby' comes from the Spanish slang word, *bubie*, meaning 'dunce'—boobies would land on the decks of sailing ships where they would be easily captured and eaten by the sailors on board. Although they are poor walkers on land, these close relatives of gannets are very graceful fliers that feed on squid and herring-like fish.

③ **Frigatebirds**

These birds are kleptoparasites—that is, they steal food from others. Frigatebirds use amazing aerial acrobatics to take food from terns, boobies and herons. They nest on several Reef islands.

① Crested terns

Many species of tern can be seen on the Great Barrier Reef, but the crested tern is one of the larger species, which is also more common. They usually nest in enormous colonies and, when the young are left on the islands to mature, they are kept in crèches tended by a few adults.

② Red-tailed tropic birds

These magnificent fliers, which are almost helpless on land, nest on several Reef islands. Their superb rosy-coloured chest feathers and long, trailing red feathers make red-tailed tropic birds some of the most spectacular species on the Great Barrier Reef.

③ Noddy terns

Two species of noddy tern nest in the Capricorn and Bunker Group at the southern end of the Reef. The common noddies nest on the ground while the black noddy species perch in flimsy nests in the trees.

Mammals

Mammals—warm-blooded, hairy animals that suckle their young—are vertebrates with strong backbones and sophisticated nervous systems.

①② Whales and dolphins

More than thirty species of dolphins and whales, are found in and near Reef waters, but the species you are most likely to see are bottle-nosed dolphins and humpback and minke whales (for more on the minke whale, see page 49). The humpback is a filter feeder with unusually long pectoral fins.

③ Dugongs

Sea cows, as dugongs are commonly called, graze the seagrass meadows throughout Great Barrier Reef waters and well beyond. They use their paddle-like forelimbs to manoeuvre themselves around wide, shallow areas. (For more information on the dugong, see page 44.)

5

FLORA AND FAUNA ON THE REEF

Major extinction events

A myriad of life forms exist on any coral reef, but to understand both them and their origins it is important to travel back to their beginnings about 3.5 billion years ago. Since life first occurred on Earth there have been five major—and perhaps twenty minor significant—extinction events. These events were due to major tectonic plate movements, meteorite strikes and massive disastrous climatic changes. It is possible to travel the world today and see old coral reefs along the tops of mountain ranges and sea floors exposed as cliff faces.

The major extinction events occurred about 440–50, 360–75, 251, 205 and 65.5 million years ago. After the third event, the largest extinction event so far recorded, the suite of organisms we can call true reef-builders—reef-building corals, twin-shelled or bivalve molluscs and coralline algae—first evolved. The final event, known as the K-T Extinction, killed off about 17 per cent of all families, 50 per cent of all genera and 75 per cent of all species during a very short geological period. Some of these events took about five million years to occur but others, such as the K-T, only a few hundred thousand years.

The K-T event occurred at the time that dinosaurs and about 33 per cent of all marine bottom-dwelling organisms became extinct;

however, some ancestors of present-day reef species survived and began a new period of speciation, surviving the minor extinction events since K-T. (Five events since then have caused the death of 50 per cent of all the faunal species on Earth today.) It was after the K-T event that both birds—in essence, modified dinosaurs—and mammals evolved as significant global inhabitants.

Species diversity needed to be high for any extinction event to have a significant impact. If you were able to look at life on Earth over the last 3.5 billion years, you would see rises and falls in species numbers—some gradual but others cataclysmic. It is due to these extinctions that about 98 per cent of the species that have been recorded are only found in the fossil record.

We can only estimate the total loss of species from the organisms that left a fossil record—many didn't—and we can only guess at the number of species currently on Earth. There is always a 'background' extinction rate occurring; this is usually due to climate change, being out-competed or eaten out by another species, and also habitat change. Since humans embarked on the Industrial Age a couple of hundred years ago, we have accelerated the background extinction rate significantly—primarily through the destruction of, and changes in, habitats.

Previous spread: A feather duster tubeworm, also known as a fan worm, is a filter feeder that retracts its tentacles when it is disturbed.

Opposite: Geikie Gorge in the Napier Range, in the Kimberley Ranges in Western Australia, is part of an ancient limestone reef.

Life under the sea

From Mount Bartle Frere—at 1622 m (5321 ft) Queensland's highest mountain—to the bottom of the Queensland Trench more than 3000 m (9842 ft) below the surface, you will discover a bewildering array of tropical and reef life. On the other side of the Queensland Trench, on the Queensland Plateau or Coral Sea Rise, the Reef becomes much shallower, which probably helped life to survive during periods of low sea stands. This is where we will look at the life to be found within and on the land, waters, reefs and sea floors surrounding the Reef.

Once you are underwater you will be immediately struck by the enormous numbers—sometimes literally a soup—of phyto (plant) and zoo (animal) plankton, which attract the larger feeding marine creatures, such as schools of small herring-like fish that, when threatened, form into what is known as a 'bait ball'. The world's biggest fish, the whale shark, as well as manta rays and thousands of smaller animals, including fish, join in the feasts offered by those grazing on the rich plankton blooms.

Left: A member of the same family as squid and octopus, the cuttlefish has three hearts and acute vision, although it cannot differentiate between colours. Like its relatives, it repels predators with ink.

The sea floor

If you drop down to the sea floor between reefs, you will enter the magical 'gardens' of occasional soft coral fans and whips, crabs, sea stars, sponge balls and craters dug by feeding fish or rays. There is an ever-passing parade of small and large animals—some are on their way to a river to spawn or out to a reef to mature, while others live here all the time. In some areas the sea floor may be almost pure mud, but in others it may be sand, coral or algal sands. If there is a rubble bottom, a base on which to live, there will often be more animals growing up into the water column to filter-feed and capture passing food.

Prawns (shrimp) lie in wait with just their eyes and spiny backs showing, waiting for prey, while Moreton Bay bugs scuttle around hunting for food. Squid and cuttlefish cruise by, changing colours to match what is below them as they wait for an unsuspecting fish to swim into range of their projectile tentacles. Scallops lie on the sea floor, filtering the water for food but, if they are disturbed or their multiple eyes around the rim of their mantle detect a threat, they will rapidly close their shells and jet away in bursts across the sea floor.

Stingrays cruise around with their electronic sensors tuned for prey buried in the sand. Once

they detect a victim, they hover over the prey in the sand and jet water down onto it, exposing the tasty morsel. On the sea floor as well as on the reef slopes and lagoon floors, you will also find several species of sea cucumber among sea stars, brittle stars and many species of molluscs.

If there are seagrass and algal beds in the back reef areas, as it begins to become shallower you will come across a stunning array of life seen by few people. Most divers call these areas 'muck diving', as they are generally muddy and less spectacular than the reefs. There are long sinuous synaptids, cousins of the sea cucumbers. One synaptid looks like a sticky, clear hollow tube with five feathery tentacles waving out of its mouth end for feeding. It often carries a pair of emperor shrimps, which keep the synaptid clear of parasites and dead tissue in exchange for some protection, the odd titbit of food and a free ride. There are also octopi that disguise themselves as hermit crabs to avoid the attention of predators but, if they are disturbed, jet off, leaving behind a cloud of black ink.

On the sea floor you may find small, hard non-reef building corals such as the popcorn coral, which settles on a small whelk shell. Then a peanut worm with a long spiky proboscis settles into the shell and drags the coral polyp around, keeping it free of the silty bottom. This is a disconcerting sight for the novice, as the worm keeps its proboscis, which looks like an elephant's trunk, hidden below the sediment, and the coral jumps about 1–2 cm (½–¾ in) as the worm retracts.

Previous spread: From time to time, concentrations of small food sources, attracted by the plankton blooms, can create baitfish balls, which will in turn attract dolphins, fish such as tuna and trevally, the filter-feeding baleen whale and, the largest fish species of all— the whale shark (pictured).

Above left: The night-feeding sticky synaptid or sea cucumber moves around some soft coral.

Above right: The peanut worm is so called because it can retract its body into a form resembling a peanut kernel.

Above left: A purple firefish swims over the rare duncan coral. Also known as the elegant firefish, this leaper will hide in holes when disturbed.

Above centre: Well camouflaged among the branching arms of an orange sea fan, a tiny pygmy seahorse feeds on plankton.

Above right: The semicircle angelfish can be found in hiding places on coastal coral reefs.

Other creatures living on the sea floor include miniature mushroom corals, fantastic free-living solitary corals with green tentacles, small black anglerfish, bizarre shrimps that look like seagrass or algae, seahorses and burrowing sea cucumbers that wave their feeding tentacles around like a mobile crown.

Giant trevally, 75 cm(2½ ft) long, come into the area, especially near dusk, and drive themselves into the sand, pumping it out through their gills as they capture their prey. In addition to all this 'big', easily seen life, there is an enormous array of small plants and animals that attach themselves to the algae and seagrasses or burrow into the sand.

Back reef slope

As you approach a reef along the sea floor from the back slope, you will usually encounter a pure sand slope that is quite unstable. Sometimes, just before you reach it, you'll pass through waving groups of garden eels, waiting for a piece of food to pass by. Once you're onto the slope, it may look reasonably sterile but if you looked through a microscope you would be amazed at the incredible array of varied life forms from many animal groups living between and on the sand grains. Many of these are yet to be 'discovered', let alone described in scientific literature.

Once you enter the back reef slope, you'll see the obvious action—the big animals and colonies are in view. If you're there at the change of shift at dawn and dusk, observing many species as they feed, hide and breed, you'll understand more of the complexities of a reef. Baitfish will hover near the reef, only to be scattered by rushing trevally as they burst through the prey, snapping up those who don't stick with the pack.

Back reef 'bommies'—isolated coral heads from a few to a hundred or so metres across—provide 'mini-reef' habitats that offer a protective environment for schools of fish. Some bommies can be made up of a single species, such as kidney coral, which may be as ancient as 2000 years old.

Right: Anthias swim around a feather star and a colony of staghorn coral on a back reef bommie.

144

Previous spread: A Queensland or giant grouper, the largest bony fish to be found on the Great Barrier Reef, swims among a school of baitfish. A huge grouper called VW lives on the SS *Yongala* shipwreck (see page 46).

Right: At low tide, when the coral is exposed, the polyps retreat inside their skeleton and secrete a protective mucus (like the purple heads pictured), which acts like a sunscreen, protecting them from the sun.

The reef top

On the reef top you enter a zone of extremes which, on most parts of the Great Barrier Reef, is subject to the ebb and flow of the tide. Here reef organisms must withstand not only predators such as sea stars, grazing parrotfish and molluscs and whatever the sea and cyclones can throw at them but also exposure to hot, dry winds, cascades of rainwater and cold, still nights, or any combination of these dangers. Nevertheless every nook and cranny is occupied, even between sand grains and upon apparently 'dead' surfaces, where many small animals occupy a rich layer of algae. During the day the pools act like small aquariums, delighting reef-walkers. At low tide, as dusk approaches, out come the night stalkers, such as octopi, ass's ear abalone, 'prawn killers' (see page 152) and eels.

On the back reef top you will find boulders, ripped off the reef during storms. If you carefully lift up one, you may see representatives of almost every animal group known to science; as space on a boulder is so limited, every protected surface is quickly occupied.

Once you are over the top of the back reef and into the lagoon, the sandy floor will seem desolate, but closer inspection will reveal a small layer of green filamentous algae on the surface. In the right light you can see a myriad of small shrimp hovering near the bottom. If you disturb the sand, you may bring to the surface crabs, shells and multitudes of small animals that cannot be seen without a microscope. As many lagoons are calm water environments, they will feature stunning colonies of delicate staghorn corals as thin as your little finger and several metres tall.

'Prawn killers' – the mantis shrimps

In the shallows it is common to find burrows up to 8 cm (3 in) across that are deep enough to hide one of the wonders of the animal kingdom—'prawn killers' or mantis shrimps, crustaceans whose front legs have been modified into either spears or clubs. The speed with which they throw these legs forward to capture prey is the fastest action known in the animal kingdom. Captured mantis shrimps have been known to shatter glass tubes and even the sides of aquariums.

Previous spread: The life forms growing on the reef crest are subjected to the full force of the prevailing weather.

Above left and centre: Some species of mantis shrimp are monogamous, and may live with the same partner for up to twenty years.

Above right: A sea urchin, which has locked itself into a crevice, is able to repel predators with its spines.

Above left: A *Pisonia* rainforest on Heron Island throws up its vertical limbs.

Above right: During the breeding season on Heron Island, wedge-tailed shearwaters fly out to sea to collect food for their young.

There may be a sand island on the reef top, created by sand and rubble that have been smashed off the reef and thrown up by the waves. First you will see the runners of goat's foot convolvulus, then spinifex or couch grasses leading into a line of horse-tail she-oaks. Behind these trees will be a forest of *Pisonia* trees with a closed canopy, and numerous burrows of wedge-tailed shearwaters underfoot, which fly in from Siberia to breed over summer. The adults feed the chicks until they are about twice their own weight, then abandon them to find their own way north. These superb fliers are quite comical on land. (See also page 131.)

It is the *Pisonia* tree's ability to reach the water in the freshwater lens (see the 'Fast Fact' at right), which allows it to grow to forest size. In these trees will be thousands of nesting black noddy terns, maintaining noise and activity twenty-four hours a day. Their nests are small, and during storms thousands of their chicks die.

Fast Fact

Rainwater filters down through the sand of coral cays and, as it is lighter than seawater, it floats, forming a pool or lens in the sand. Where the freshwater lens meets the seawater on the beach, beachrock is formed, cemented together by the calcium carbonate dissolved in the freshwater. Old beach lines can be seen, as these soft rocks run at different angles on some cays.

Fast Fact

Millions of tonnes of force are expended on the reef fronts almost daily and, when you see the shape of the surface, you can understand why the plants and animals that live here need to be so robust.

Left: A single surgeonfish swims over a coral reef beneath a breaking wave on a reef crest. Sometimes these fish can be found swimming in schools but they are usually solitary.

The seaward reef top

Moving onto the seaward reef top, you will be faced once again with an array of small aquarium-like pools that lead onto an almost solid concrete-like surface. On the reefs in the south this reef crest is a combination of mussels and turf algae, some of which look like grasses. In the north, coralline or red algae and coral colonies tend to protect the reef top by taking the brunt of the seaward side of the reef.

Moving deeper, over the front edge of the reef, the coral colonies can afford to be a little larger—until a cyclone comes along and rips them off—and more fish are seen. Off the outer edge or windward area of a shelf edge reef, the water quality from the nearby ocean can allow some corals to survive to greater depths than inshore. Some of the plate coral colonies reach up to 5 m (16½ ft) across as they strive to grow into more light. As in all parts of the reef, the slow-growing massive corals may be overshadowed by these faster-growing species. However, generally the slow-growing corals are better attached and more likely to survive cyclonic waves than the fast-growing plate corals.

Further down the reef slope are enormous fans of soft corals, accompanied by their cousins, the whips and comb species; at this depth there is insufficient light for hard corals and algae to grow.

The ocean depths

Little is known of the species that live down in the darker depths of the ocean, where terraces indicate periods of wave action some time in the past. At about 300 m (984 ft) down, it is possible to trap nautilus shells—primitive molluscs adapted for life in the deep. In 1938 a coelacanth, known only from the fossil record, was caught off the east coast of Africa, about 400–600 m (1312–1968 ft) below sea level. Since then more have been discovered in Indonesia; perhaps they also live in the waters around Australia.

At these depths there are giant squid and octopi, sea stars, brittle stars and crabs not affected by the pressure, as well as all sorts of bizarre fish and other animals with bioluminescent systems, which enable them to emit light to attract prey or mates.

The search goes on. We know more about the Moon and outer space than we do about the depths of our oceans.

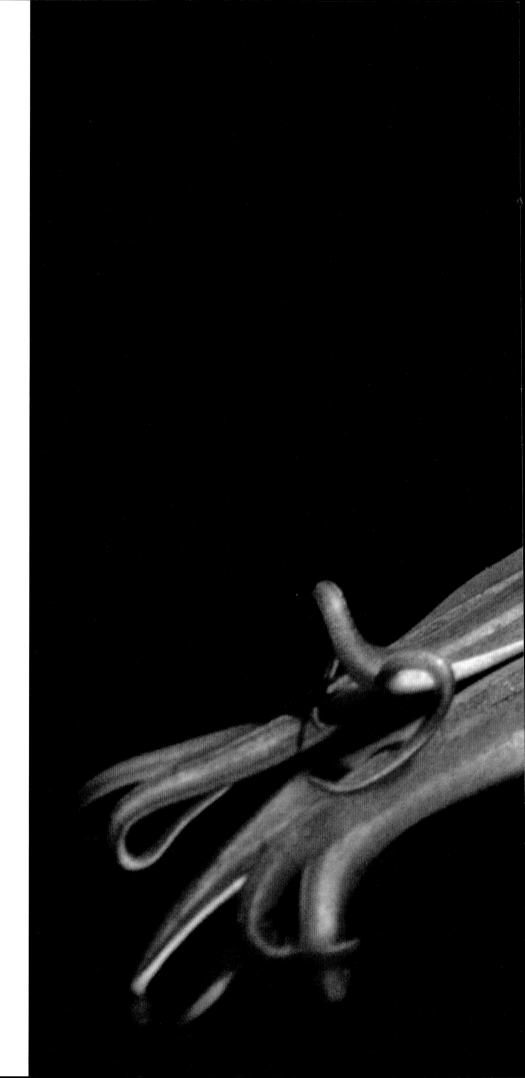

Right: A humboldt or jumbo squid at night. This aggressive, predatory squid can swim in groups of more than 1200.

Left: An epaulette shark hunts in shallow water off Lizard Island. This predator is specially adapted to hunt among the coral at low tide. It can 'walk' on its front fins as well as increase the blood supply to its brain so it can survive longer without breathing.

Sharks

The waters surrounding the reef are constantly patrolled by many species of fish, including sharks. The sedentary species stay in one area only, while the pelagic species, which live in the open ocean, are opportunistic feeders, just passing by. We do not know how many sharks live in and around the Great Barrier Reef waters today, nor do we have reliable past or present statistics. In the early 1970s, divers entering the waters of the Reef on the outer edge of the shelf would see at least several black reef sharks and one or two silver-tip sharks as they entered the water. This does not happen today. Black-tip reef sharks were also once very common but it is now rare to see one. Bigger species of sharks —such as tiger, bull, whalers and the like—have all declined in number and size. There is no fishing restriction on sharks, so this could contribute to the decline in numbers.

In the coastal rainforests you might find cassowaries, large and extremely shy flightless birds that will deliver a mighty kick when threatened. They eat fruit, spreading the seeds.

Air-breathing animals

Air-breathing animals—such as birds, turtles and sea snakes—represent a link with the species that live only underwater.

Birds

Although birds are important players in reef life, they are often forgotten. They are superb in the air and many can also 'fly' underwater. There are also those species—such as egrets, waders and fish-eaters—that operate between the air and the fish in the water. You will find birds in every habitat on the reef, taking life and using it to grow or feed their young. Mangrove muds, seagrasses at low tide and exposed reef tops all provide rich pickings.

Birds stabilise sand cays, carrying seeds from the mainland to the islands (or from island to island), maintaining ecological balances on many islands, preventing overpopulation of some species of prey and depositing guano to help the growth of plant communities on the cays.

Birds also transport seeds and various organic materials from other habitats adjacent to the Reef onto islands with a similar climate. Some species of island plants, such as *Pisonia* trees, have a sticky seed bunch that can trap a bird. An exhausted bird may float to a nearby island, where it dies. The seeds germinate, helped along by a dose of fertiliser provided by the dead body.

Right: An adult brown booby and chick. The female lays two eggs in a nest on the ground. As the chicks grow, the stronger one will throw the weaker one out of the nest.

① Juvenile brown booby
② Crested terns
③ Wedge-tailed shearwater
④ Pied oystercatcher
⑤ Eastern reef egret
⑥ Frigatebird
⑦ Black noddy
⑧ Silver gulls
⑨ Red-tailed tropic bird

Floating 'habitats'

Floating objects such as logs, plastic buoys, sawn
timber, pumice rafts from volcanic eruptions and
even crocodiles will be found well out to sea and
throughout Great Barrier Reef waters. They may
wash up on the coast or islands. Depending on how
long they have been at sea, they will be covered in
an array of marine life and used as a perch for
resting birds. Thousands of algal species and
animals, including barnacles, worms, crabs, sponges,
lace corals and corals, will encrust these floating
'habitats'. The larger the object, the greater the
number of organisms it will support, including small
fish larvae or adults who graze on the attached life.
These in turn attract bigger fish, and so on, up the
predatory chain.

Fast Fact

Many species of fruit- and seed-eaters roost on
islands but feed on the mainland, so each night the
birds carry back a load of seeds that, mixed with their
droppings, transport plant species out to the islands.

Above: Pumice is a porous
volcanic rock, full of bubbles,
which is light enough to float on
water. Some pumice rafts can be
as large as 30 km (18 mi) across.
Here, at the top of the tide line,
you can see the remains of
sponges and worm tubes.

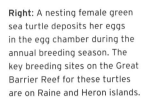

Right: A nesting female green sea turtle deposits her eggs in the egg chamber during the annual breeding season. The key breeding sites on the Great Barrier Reef for these turtles are on Raine and Heron islands.

Far right: Green sea turtle hatchlings make their way from the nest to the sea. Years later they will return to the same place to breed.

Fast Fact

Some species of turtle and many other creatures on the Reef often die after ingesting plastic bags. The turtles mistake the bags for sea jellies, which is a source of food.

Turtles

Turtles are among the most ancient animals on the planet, yet they have a life cycle we did not fully understand until recently. They spend most of their lives at sea, and each year up to tens of thousands of turtles will come ashore to lay their eggs on Great Barrier Reef islands or nearby coastlines. Male turtles hang around nesting spots so they can mate with a female only days before she lays her eggs. She can store this sperm for years.

After about 5–12 weeks, depending on the sand conditions, the eggs hatch. The temperature in the middle of the nest determines the sex of the young, with males in the cooler range (26°C/79°F) and females in the warmer range (30°C/86°F).

If the young survive the journey from the nest to the water, they can swim freely for some years, doing a circuit of the South Pacific, travelling as far as the coast of South America before returning as sub-adults, long before they become sexually mature at thirty years of age or more.

While they are on the open ocean, turtles feed on planktonic organisms but, once they return to Great Barrier Reef waters, depending on the species, they forage on mud and sand flats, seagrass beds, algal turf areas and on coral reefs.

Most turtle species remain in a relatively small foraging 'home range', although others have been known to swim thousands of kilometres to and from feeding grounds between breeding cycles. Each breeding cycle varies from three to eight layings in one year, with three to five years between each cycle.

Coastal urbanisation affects laying turtles and hatchling success, and warmer northern beaches are becoming less suitable for turtle nests. Rising temperatures due to climate change are resulting in more females being born.

Previous spread: A green sea turtle hatchling, having survived hunting birds such as the rufus night heron on its journey from the nest to the sea, swims in open water, where it may become prey to sharks and other large fish.

Left: An olive sea snake cruises over the SS *Yongala* shipwreck (see page 46). The snake has one cylindrical lung that is almost as long as its body.

Sea snakes

Sea snakes are, in essence, the same as land snakes, but their bodies are flattened sideways rather than vertically. Some of the most venomous snake species on the planet, they rarely use their venom, and when they do it is usually for feeding. They regularly breathe air at the surface, although they can remain underwater for up to two hours at a time. Depending on whether they are in a feeding or resting cycle, which can last from twenty minutes to two hours, they may sunbake on the surface for a while. Sea snakes feed on fish, fish eggs, crabs and other easily caught meals.

6
EXPERIENCING THE REEF

Respecting the rules

If you can do it in, on or near the water, you can probably do it on the Great Barrier Reef. Some Reef tourist activities are found nowhere else in the world.

But whatever you do, or wherever you go on the Reef, please ensure your activities comply with the GBRMPA Zoning Plans. These are freely available online, at all the resorts, on all the charter and tour boats, or by mail. And there are many ways to reach the islands of your choice—from sailboats, slow boats, fast catamarans and monohulls to helicopters, amphibious aircraft, floatplanes and commercial jets.

While much of this chapter is based on the GBRMPA and Queensland Marine Parks websites, their Zoning Plans and rules change from time to time, so it is essential to familiarise yourself with them before you venture into the Great Barrier Reef Marine Park or National Park islands on your own.

The tourist operators who take you out on the Reef should always explain what is not allowed in the area you are visiting. Most of these people are dedicated 'reefies', but if they don't explain the rules to you, just ask them exactly what limitations, if any, apply to your activities during your visit. You will enjoy a successful and safe experience if you treat the whole area as one big national park. The Great Barrier Reef is a Marine Park with many zones allowing all sorts of activities, but there are also some totally closed areas with severe restrictions and penalties.

Previous spread: Scuba diving allows visitors to explore reef slopes and drop-offs.

Opposite: Visiting the Great Barrier Reef can entail more than exploring the coral reefs. A pool in a rainforest provides a tranquil retreat.

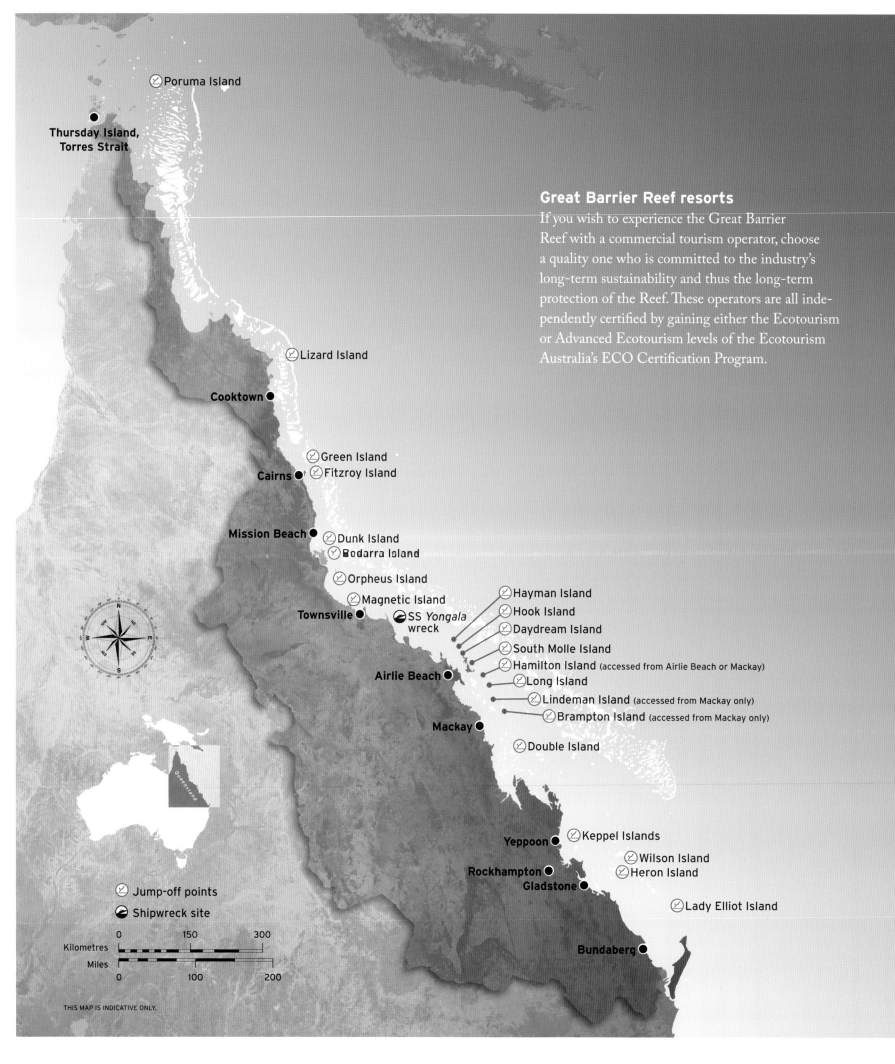

Poruma Island

Thursday Island,
Torres Strait

Great Barrier Reef resorts

If you wish to experience the Great Barrier
Reef with a commercial tourism operator, choose
a quality one who is committed to the industry's
long-term sustainability and thus the long-term
protection of the Reef. These operators are all inde-
pendently certified by gaining either the Ecotourism
or Advanced Ecotourism levels of the Ecotourism
Australia's ECO Certification Program.

Lizard Island

Cooktown

Green Island

Cairns   Fitzroy Island

Mission Beach   Dunk Island
Bedarra Island

Orpheus Island

Magnetic Island   Hayman Island

Townsville   SS *Yongala*   Hook Island
wreck   Daydream Island

South Molle Island

Hamilton Island (accessed from Airlie Beach or Mackay)

Airlie Beach   Long Island

Lindeman Island (accessed from Mackay only)

Brampton Island (accessed from Mackay only)

Mackay

Double Island

Keppel Islands

Yeppoon

Wilson Island

Rockhampton   Heron Island

Gladstone

Lady Elliot Island

Jump-off points

Shipwreck site

Bundaberg

Kilometres
| 0 | 150 | 300 |

Miles
| 0 | 100 | 200 |

THIS MAP IS INDICATIVE ONLY.

Jump-off point	Resort	Type of island	How to get there
Thursday Island, Torres Strait	Poruma or Coconut Island	Coral cay	Light aircraft/twins
Cooktown	Lizard Island	Mainland island	Light aircraft/twins
Cairns	Green Island	Coral cay	Fast boat/helicopter
	Fitzroy Island	Mainland island	Fast boat
	Lizard Island	Mainland island	Light aircraft/twins
Mission Beach	Dunk Island	Mainland island	Boat/light aircraft
	Beddarra Island	Mainland island	Boat
Townsville	Bedarra Island	Mainland island	Boat
	Orpheus Island	Mainland island	Amphibian/boat
	Magnetic Island	Mainland island	Fast boat
Airlie Beach or Hamilton Island	Hamilton Island	Mainland island	Jet/fast boat
	Long Island	Mainland island	Fast boat
	South Molle Island	Mainland island	Fast boat
	Daydream Island	Mainland island	Fast boat
	Hayman Island	Mainland island	Jet, then fast boat
Mackay	Brampton Island	Mainland island	Fast boat
	Lindeman Island	Mainland island	Boat/light aircraft
	Hamilton Island	Mainland island	Jet/fast boat
Yeppoon/Rockhampton	Keppel Islands	Mainland island	Fast boat
Gladstone	Heron Island	Coral cay	Helicopter/fast boat
	Wilson Island		
Bundaberg	Lady Elliot Island	Coral rubble/sand cay	Light aircraft

Possession Island

**Thursday Island,
Torres Strait**

⛺ Flinders Group of Islands

⛺ Nymph Island
⛺ Lizard Island
⛺ Turtle Group of Islands
⛺ Two Isles
⛺ Three Isles
⛺ East Hope Islands

Cooktown ●

⛺ Frankland Islands

Cairns ●

⛺ Family Islands Group

⛺ Barnard Islands Group

Mission Beach ●
⛺ Goold Island
Cardwell ●
⛺ Hinchinbrook Island
Lucinda ●
⛺ Orpheus Island
⛺ Magnetic Island

Townsville ●

⛺ Holbourne Island
⛺ Whitsunday Islands
Airlie Beach ●
⛺ Lindeman Islands Group
⛺ Newry Islands Group
⛺ Carlisle Island
Mackay ●
⛺ Northumberland Islands Group
⛺ Percy Islands

⛺ Tyron Island
⛺ Northwest Island
⛺ Keppel Islands
Yeppoon ●
⛺ Curtis Island
Rockhampton ●
⛺ Lady Musgrave Island
Gladstone ●

⛺ Camping sites

Bundaberg ●

Kilometres
0   150

Miles
0   100

THIS MAP IS INDICATIVE ONLY.

Camping on the Great Barrier Reef

You can camp on many National Park islands of the
Reef (for permits and information, see page 240).
Most are part of the Great Barrier Reef World
Heritage Area. For a list of camping sites, see the
table opposite. You may be able to visit and camp or
stay on several islands within Torres Strait, but you
must contact the Torres Strait Regional Authority
(see page 240).

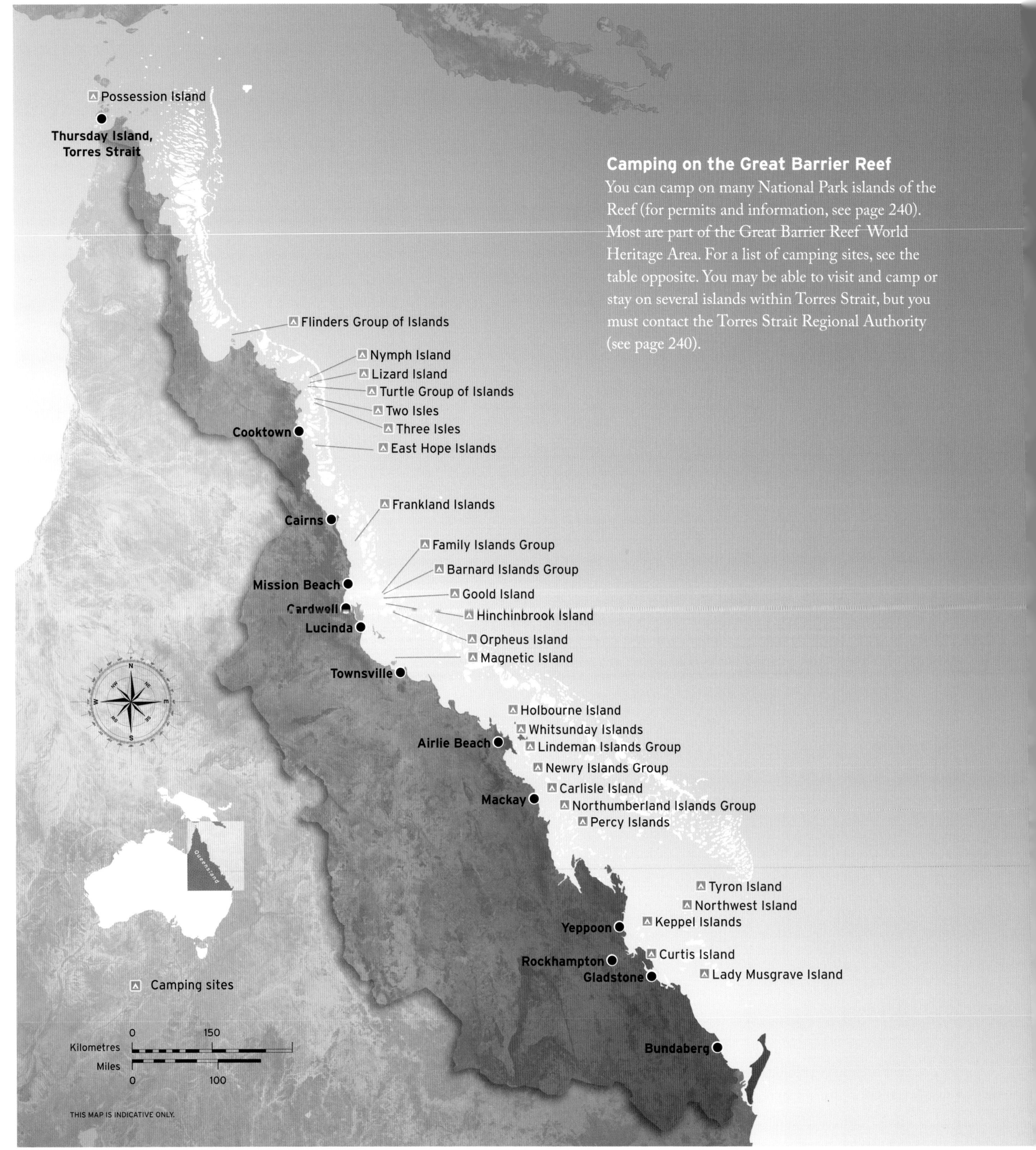

Queensland National Park island camping sites

Camping site	Type of island	How to get there	Jump-off point
Possession Island	Mainland island	Boat	Cooktown
Flinders Group of Islands	Mainland islands	Boat	Cooktown
Nymph Island	Rubble/shingle cay	Boat	Cooktown
Lizard Island (2 sites)	Mainland island	Air	Cairns
Turtle Group of Islands (3 sites)	Rubble/shingle cays	Boat	Cooktown
Two Isles	Sand cay	Boat	Cooktown
Three Isles (2 sites)	Coral cay	Boat	Cooktown
East Hope Island	Coral cay	Boat	Cooktown
Frankland Islands	Mainland islands	Boat	Mission Beach or nearby coast
Family Islands Group – Bowden Island, Coombe Island, Dunk Island and Wheeler Island	Mainland islands	Boat	Cardwell
Barnard Islands Group – Hutchison Island, Kent Island and Stephens Island	Mainland islands	Boat	Cairns or nearby coast
Goold Island	Mainland island	Boat	Cardwell
Hinchinbrook Island (10 campsites based primarily along the superb Thorsbourne Trail)	Mainland island	Boat	Cardwell or Lucinda
Orpheus Island (4 sites)	Mainland island	Boat	Townsville or Taylors Beach
Magnetic Island	Mainland island	Fast ferry	Townsville
Holbourne Island	Mainland island	Boat	Airlie Beach or nearby coast
Whitsunday Islands (61 camping spots on various islands)	Mainland islands	Many forms of transport	Airlie Beach
Lindeman Islands Group (13 sites)	Mainland islands	Fast boat	Mackay or Lindeman Island
Newry Islands Group (3 sites)	Mainland islands	Boat	Mackay or Airlie Beach
Carlisle Island	Mainland island	Boat	Mackay or Brampton Island
Northumberland Islands Group (3 sites)	Mainland islands	Boat	Mackay or Airlie Beach
Percy Islands	Mainland island	Boat	Mackay or Brampton Island
Tryon Island	Sand cay	Barge or fast boat	Yeppoon or Gladstone
Northwest Island	Sand cay	Barge or fast boat	Yeppoon or Gladstone
Keppel Bay Islands – Conical, Corroboree, Divided, Halfway, Humpy, Masthead, Miall, Middle, North Keppel, Peak and Pelican Islands	Mainland islands	Fast boat	Yeppoon
Curtis Island	Mainland island	Boat	Gladstone
Lady Musgrave Island	Sand cay	Fast boat	Bundaberg or Town of 1770

If you have a permit to camp on a Great Barrier Reef island, usually all the beachside and boating activities are available to you. Seasonal closures apply to some islands, and some activities may be restricted or prohibited. You may encounter Marine Park and Researcher personnel—please do not interrupt them unless you are invited—but a real bonus might be coming across the operator of a commercial fishing vessel anchored nearby who is willing to sell you fresh seafood.

At all times, protect the islands and reefs, as they are fragile and easily damaged. Check the relevant Zoning Plan for restrictions on line fishing and collecting shells. Both collecting coral and spearfishing using scuba gear are prohibited.

Above: Pontoons – which may include an underwater observatory and scuba diving platforms as well as dining facilities – are a great way to experience the Great Barrier Reef.

Right: A broken staghorn coral, damaged by storms, fish or even divers.

Far right: Turtles can easily mistake a plastic bag for food, so never leave rubbish behind on the Reef.

Here are some specific points to note.

- Do not feed the gulls. The numbers of gulls are increasing on many Reef islands, and when they appear, the other birds take off from their nests, resulting in a quick death for the exposed egg or chick (see also page 131).
- If you come by boat, avoid coral damage by dropping your anchor in sand or mud. Use a lightweight reef pick with plastic tubing over the anchor chain.
- Do not bring pets. They are not allowed.
- Never get too close to nesting seabirds (again, see page 131).
- Stay on any walking tracks. If you collapse a shearwater's nesting tunnel, you can not only injure yourself but also trap the young inside. If that happens, dig them out by hand.
- Don't use white lights on beaches during the turtle-breeding season from late October to April. Instead, use only red or yellow lights and fuel stoves, as white lights and fires attract and kill birds as well as turtle hatchlings.
- Open fires are rarely allowed. Do not collect any firewood.
- When reef walking, do not disturb the animals (see page 181).
- If there are no toilets, bury human waste beyond high tide level. Never bury rubbish.

- Don't throw it, stow it. Dumping plastic and other rubbish at sea is illegal, and can harm or kill aquatic animals. Take all your rubbish back to the mainland. You can dump unwanted food scraps that will easily biodegrade as long as you are more than 500 m (547 yd) beyond the reef edge, but do not dispose of more durable scraps such as corn cobs and orange peels.

Be prepared

Here are some tips on how to protect yourself when you visit the Great Barrier Reef.

- Few islands have either fresh water or facilities, so take everything you need. Allow 5 L (1 gal) of water a day for each person. Take extra supplies for a minimum of three days in case you become stranded by sudden changes in the weather.
- Be alert to sudden weather changes, particularly storms and cyclones. Be prepared to evacuate if necessary.
- Be aware of tidal variations and strong currents. Anchor boats securely.
- Carry a marine band radio transceiver and satellite phone. Most Reef sites are out of range for mobile phones.
- Always wear a broad-brimmed hat, long-sleeved shirt and sunscreen.

Left: If you explore a reef at low tide you might see stinging hydroids, which look a little like collections of ferns but have tentacles that can give you an itchy rash.

Reef walking

At low tide many reefs will be exposed, and it is a privilege to be able to walk on them, but take special care to protect both the Reef and yourself. Make sure you only land and walk on a robust reef surface, then follow these precautions.

- Plan your walk to follow the low tide out, then head back just before low tide is reached. Make sure you know how to read that area's charts.
- Wear thick-soled shoes and long pants or socks. Lycra suits are ideal, as they protect you from the sun, stingers, cuts and abrasions.
- Use a bucket or container with a clear base for easy underwater viewing.
- Many dangerous animals—including cone shells, stinging hydroids and stonefish—live on the Great Barrier Reef. They can inject toxins that can cause serious injury or even death, so avoid picking up, touching or treading on any marine life. Only a qualified guide or someone with a good knowledge of marine biology can advise you on what is safe.
- Move along sand channels and avoid stepping on, and killing, any coral or sea life. At all times stay in the shallows, less than knee-deep. Avoid the fragile corals on the edges of pools and channels.
- If you're on a marked trail, follow the markers. Never stray off the trail or take shortcuts.
- If there is no marked trail, take time to locate any regularly used trails.
- If you turn over a boulder to investigate the life beneath it, keep it wet at all times and make sure you carefully return it to its original position.

Right: A scuba diver explores a reef drop-off encrusted with soft corals such as red, pink and yellow dendronephthya as well as whip corals, all providing protection for a school of baitfish.

Snorkelling and diving

There are many superb places on the Great Barrier Reef where you can snorkel and dive; however, in a few places you'll need a Marine Park permit. Check the Zoning Plan for that area before you go. For your own safety, and to protect the Reef, be careful when diving and snorkelling around coral. Also be aware that it is common to come across a reef that has been recently decimated by crown-of-thorns sea stars, coral bleaching or cyclones.

Safety

In Australia, the basic requirement for recreational divers is a current, open-water scuba diving certificate that has been issued by a recognised, accredited diving organisation, such as PADI, SSI or NAUI. If you haven't dived for some time, take a refresher dive with a dive master or local dive school before you visit the Reef. Before snorkelling on the Reef, take lessons from an experienced person, such as a qualified scuba diving instructor, and practise in safe, shallow water. Be aware of strong currents around the islands, and stay away from areas where boats operate.

The best advice is to look, don't touch. Some marine organisms can deliver painful, dangerous or even fatal stings.

Right: Game fishing is a popular activity on the Great Barrier Reef. Here recreational fishers haul in a black marlin.

Fishing in Great Barrier Reef waters

The Reef offers a wonderfully diverse range of fishing locations and types of fish to catch. However, many areas are totally closed to fishing, so make sure you know about these before you head out. The closed areas act as 'supply depots' for new fish so the gaps in overfished areas can be filled.

As the total fish catch has doubled in the last thirty years, it is imperative that you do what you can to let fish stocks regenerate—hence GBRMPA's introduction of closed areas as well as size and bag limits. Have fun, but please only take what you really need and release as many as possible, then enjoy the great catches when you come back next time. There are protected species too, and the penalties for catching these can be quite severe.

If you do catch a tagged fish, record the tag details and let the fish go (see 'Returning unwanted fish', page 186). Report the details to the hotline (see page 240) and you will be surprised by the history of the fish that you held for those few moments. Should you see any illegal fishing or large fish kills, please also report them to the appropriate hotline (see page 240).

*   Do not use pest or non-native fish for bait or release introduced species into the water. Please do not fish where fish feeding takes place—for example, as part of a tourist program.
*   If you're unsure of the identity or legal size of the fish, release it immediately. Release all undersized and unwanted fish quickly to minimise injury.
*   If you plan to keep the fish, remove it from the hook or net immediately and kill it in a humane way. Before you head home, clean up all your fishing gear (such as bait bags and discarded tackle and line) and take it back to shore so you can dispose of it properly. Also keep in mind that in some areas you must have all your fishing gear stowed, even if you are just passing through.

Dangerous fins

The majority of divers and snorkellers cause little noticeable damage to corals; most damage that does occur results from fins. If you are inexperienced, try to practise snorkelling away from living coral. Be aware of where your fins are, and avoid touching anything with them. Never rest or stand on coral. If you must stand up, do so on sand, or use rest stations. Your body will float easily, especially with a snorkel tube connecting you to the surface. Before meeting the fish, practise until you are comfortable.

Spearfishing

Spearfishing can be an excellent challenge, but only spear what you need, and certainly do not pursue a fish if you are unsure of its identity or legal size. Big fish are important breeding stock, so don't take them merely as trophies.

Spearfishing while wearing scuba gear is prohibited. If you are spearfishing while using snorkel gear, be very careful near others. You must check the Zoning Plan to see where spearfishing is allowed. Spearguns are not allowed in a national park without written authority unless they have been dismantled and securely stored in a boat.

Practise shooting and aiming on a target on a sandy patch, for example, before you go for a fish because, if you miss it, it's almost impossible to get the spear out of the coral without unscrewing the head. Spearguns have a unique kick-up, which results in many missed or injured targets. Make sure you track down injured fish rather than let them swim off to die a slow death.

Returning unwanted fish

Always minimise the length of time a fish is out of the water and have your equipment close at hand. Do not remove very large fish from the water, and do not leave smaller fish on a hot, dry surface to thrash around, as this can destroy their very delicate protective mucous coating. Place them on a wet towel and cover them, especially their gills and eyes, which can be damaged by the sun.

Handle the fish gently with wet hands and a wet cloth, fully supporting its body. Do not hold it upright by the jaw, squeeze it or kneel on it. Using a pair of long-nose pliers or a de-hooker to minimise tissue tearing, remove the hook carefully and quickly. If the hook is difficult to remove, cut the line instead. Even better, buy the new easy-release hooks, barbless hooks or any type that is unlikely to become hooked in the gills or gut.

Finally, help the fish to recover before you release it—hold it head first into the current and when it starts to swim away, let it go.

Opposite: A typical spearfisher's catch might include crayfish, coral trout, wrasse, sweetlips and parrotfish.

Right: A pair of black noddy terns on Lady Elliot Island. These birds build their nests on platforms in the trees, and will return to the same island in the next breeding season.

Birdwatching

With an estimated 175 bird species, the Great Barrier Reef Marine Park boasts an incredible collection of birdlife. Some are year-round residents, while thousands of others use the Marine Park as a pit stop on their exhausting annual migration.

Many of the Reef's islands are internationally significant breeding and nesting sites and offer an amazing wildlife experience. The birds are particularly vulnerable during nesting and it's vital you take special care not to disturb them. Slight disturbances may scare an adult bird off its nest, and it can take only minutes for unattended eggs to become overheated, or for gulls to eat them or the chicks.

Also bear in mind the following advice.

- Land and launch your boat well away from any seabirds or shorebirds.
- Do not pull your dinghy up the beach into nesting areas.
- Watch your step to avoid crushing camouflaged eggs and chicks, and never try to touch birds, chicks or eggs.
- Stay well clear of nesting and roosting shorebirds and seabirds. Keep quiet, move slowly in a crouched position and use existing cover. If you notice any birds being disturbed, back off and go elsewhere—as mentioned above, the gulls are adept at stealing the eggs and chicks.
- Do not sound horns, claxons, sirens or loudspeakers. Muffle the sound of your anchor chain.
- Do not shine torches or bright lights directly on roosting or nesting seabirds. Instead, angle the lights to the side, and cover bulbs with red cellophane or filters.

Enjoying the natural world of the Reef

For the best Great Barrier Reef experience, go out
with an open mind and, ideally, guide books on the
fish, birds and marine life, or consult the reading list
on page 238 for several fantastic guides. Equipped
with binoculars and a child-like curiosity, you will
be astounded by what you discover, all without
moving more than 100 m (109 yd) from your base.
By expecting the unexpected, you will never be
disappointed by the Great Barrier Reef.

Above: You can take an airborne scenic tour of the Great Barrier Reef, or explore its pristine waters on a yacht.

The Traditional Owners

About 100,000–50,000 years ago, Aboriginals moved onto the dry northeastern coastal plain of the Australian continent, possibly via a land bridge that once connected Indonesia and Papua New Guinea with Australia. Here they would have hunted and gathered among the thousands of flat-topped limestone hills that now make up the Great Barrier Reef, and also off the continental shelf, down to about 130 m (426 ft) below the current sea level.

Over a period of 18,000 to 6000 years ago, the sea gradually rose to its present level, forcing the Aboriginal people off the shelf and onto the coastal plain. Perhaps this last rapid rise of water was 'the great flood' described in many ancient texts and recorded by indigenous people in many cultures all over the world.

According to one theory, the colonisation of Australia by Europeans, who settled on the continent in 1788, led to the demise of the majority of the Aboriginal population—up to 90 per cent died from diseases against which they had no resistance. Of the remaining 10 per cent, many were killed off either by poisoned waterholes or 'dispersal' shooting parties formed by graziers, who continued this practice until the late 1890s and, in some areas, well into the twentieth century.

Of a population of about 48,000 Torres Strait Islanders, some 6000 now live on the islands; the rest live on the Australian mainland, primarily in Townsville and Cairns. These sea-faring people of Melanesian origin moved into the islands of Torres Strait approximately 2500 years ago. They supplemented agriculture with hunting and gathering and, with their fierce war-like behaviour and sea-faring skills, dominated the neighbouring Australian Aboriginal and Papuan cultures.

European exploration

According to Portuguese naval records, the first Europeans to discover Australia were Cristóvão de Mendonça, in 1522, and Gomes de Sequeira, in 1525. As both men had ventured into what was then the Spanish half of the known world, their discovery was kept secret to prevent incurring papal wrath and excommunication.

There is no doubt that the Portuguese were in Timorese waters around this time, but what records were kept—fabricated and modified by French and other European mariners, for example—are now all regarded with scepticism by historians. When the coastline at the bottom of the Dauphin Map (see page 198), drawn between 1530 and 1536, is transposed to today's Mercator projection, it bears a strong resemblance to Australia; however, the same claim can also be made for the coast of Indo-China.

Willem Janszoon followed the Portuguese on the Dutch East India Company ship, the *Duyfken*, and came ashore on the west coast of Cape York

Jave La Grande

An 1856 copy of a map from a 1547 atlas, one of the Dieppe Maps, this Portuguese map of Jave La Grande or 'great island of Java', presumed to be the largest island in the world at the time, accurately marks geographical sites along the east coast of Cape York Peninsula, proving that Portuguese adventurers discovered this coast almost 250 years before the British sailed into Botany Bay in 1770. To compare it with a modern map, turn it upside down.

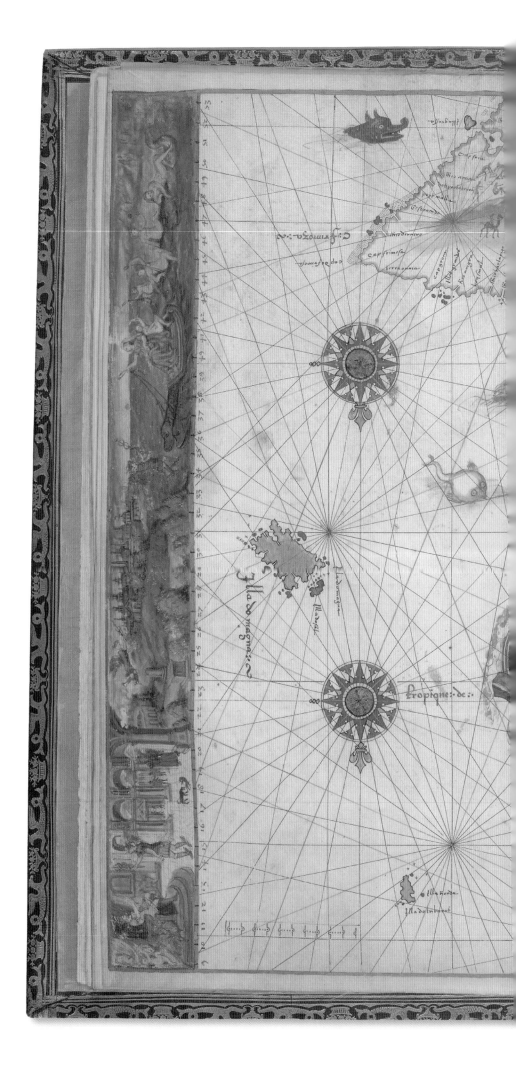

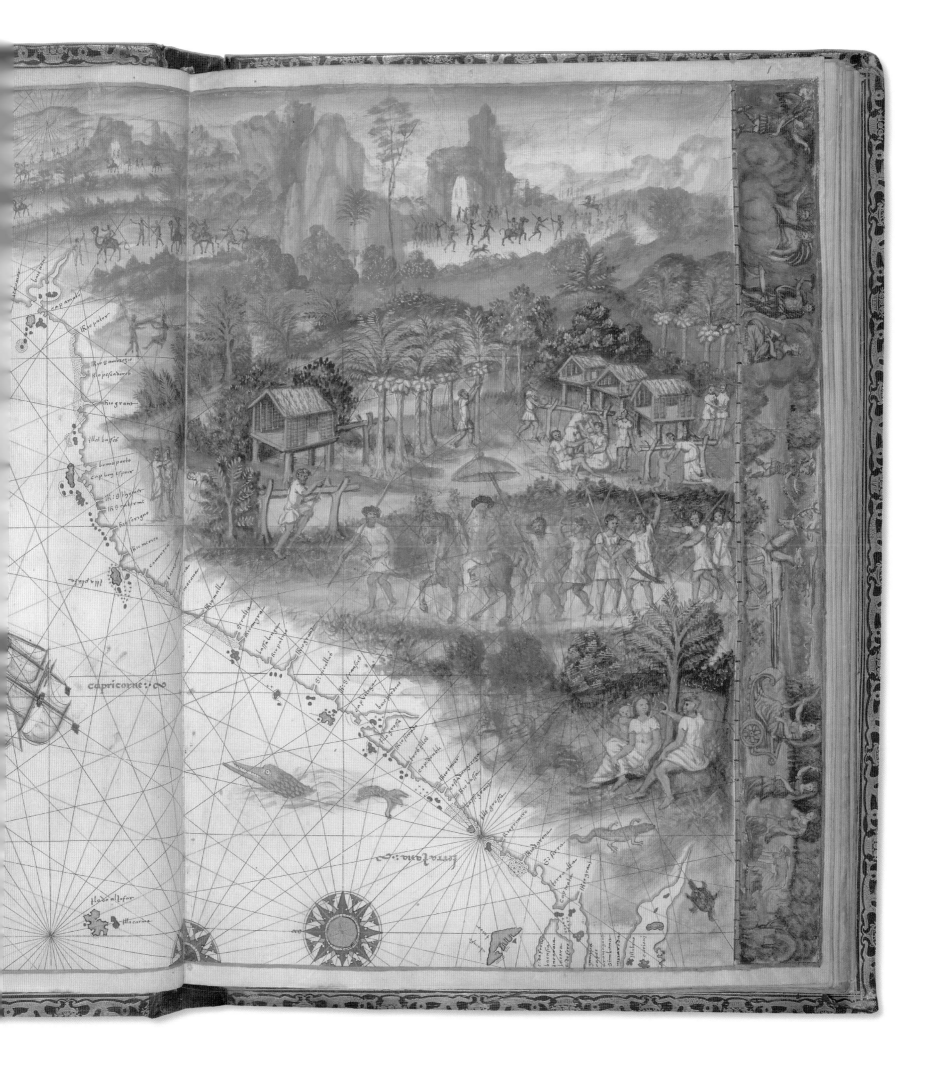

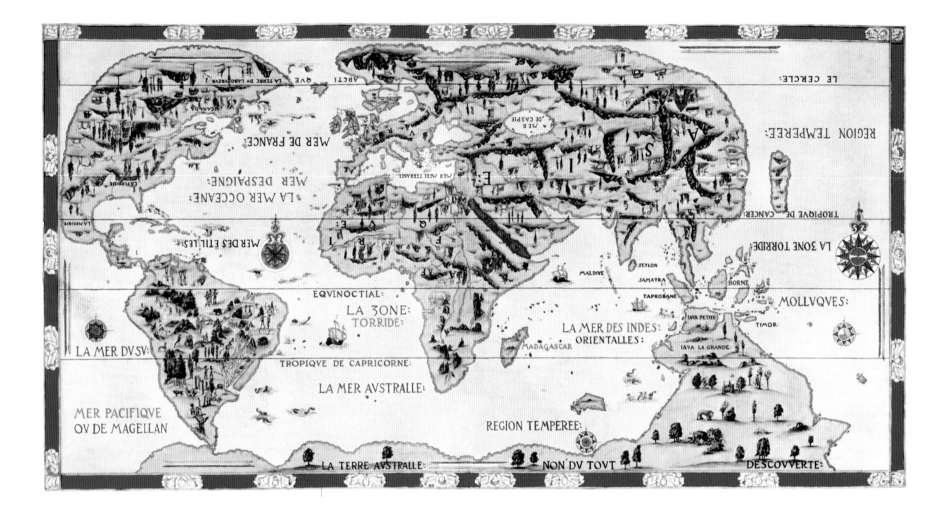

Fast Fact

To seventeenth century Dutch mariners, the newly discovered coasts were known as the unknown lands 'east of Banda', irresistible to those who imagined the new lands were part of the theoretical, almost legendary 'Great South Land'.

Above: The Dauphin map, drawn between 1530 and 1536 by Portugese mariners. While naval records suggest the first Europeans to discover Australia were Cristóvão de Mendonça and Gomes de Sequeira, their discovery was kept secret to prevent incurring papal wrath and excommunication.

near the Pennefather River in February 1606. His voyage is the earliest firmly documented sighting of Australia. Janszoon charted the west coast of Cape York Peninsula, thus launching forty years of Dutch maritime exploration in Australian waters.

In 1623 more confusion resulted from the voyages of the Dutch ships, *Pera* and the *Arnhem*: the *Pera* chart clearly shows a wide gap between Cape York and New Guinea between 9° and 10°S, whereas the *Arnhem* chart shows the Cape York coast as a continuation of the New Guinea coast. However, a Spanish ship, commanded by Luís Vaz de Torres, had already secretly passed through the

strait from the South Pacific in 1606. The Spanish captain had sighted the islands of Torres Strait while sailing from east to west along the southern coast of Papua, which he claimed for the Spanish in late 1606. It is believed he may have entered Reef waters as far south as Endeavour Strait before sailing north, through the strait that now bears his name. Alexander Dalrymple, the first British naval hydrographer, saw the accounts of Torres' expedition while he was translating documents captured in the Philippines in 1762. He gave a sketch map of the voyage to Joseph Banks, who brought it to the attention of James Cook (see opposite).

Above left: Even when equipped with modern navigational instruments, ships still run aground on Endeavour Reef.

Above centre: Alexander Huey, *Portrait of Rear-Admiral William Bligh*, 1814, watercolour on ivory, 11.5 x 8.4 cm. Bligh was the first to supply the semblance of an accurate chart of the east coast of Cape York peninsular north of Restoration Island.

Above right: The replica of HMS *Bounty*. The ship was originally a three-masted cargo ship but was modified to be used for the botanical expedition under Bligh's leadership in 1787.

In April 1789, after Lieutenant William Bligh was deposed by mutineers on board HMS *Bounty*, he was set adrift in a longboat with eighteen crew. Equipped only with basic navigation instruments, minimal supplies and a good memory, Bligh struck out for Timor. He guided the boat onto the Great Barrier Reef through what is now known as Bligh's Passage, then to Restoration Island and up the east coast, through Torres Strait to Timor. By Bligh's calculations the forty-seven-day journey covered some 6710 km (3618 nautical miles).

The next Europeans who were known to be in the Great Barrier Reef area were on board HMS *Pandora* as it attempted to make its way into the Reef. After running aground, it sank on 29 August 1791, with four of the fourteen *Bounty* mutineers, whom Captain Edwards had captured in Tahiti, and thirty-one of the 120 crew. The remaining ten mutineers and eighty-nine crew spent several days on a sand cay just inside what is now known as Pandora Entrance. Once the longboats had been prepared, Edwards and his fellow survivors made their way to Timor and, eventually, England.

Meanwhile, on 2 August 1791, Bligh had set out from England on HMS *Providence*, on his second breadfruit voyage. Due to the difficulty of sailing among the reefs and shoals from the 'Great North East Channel', it took him about two weeks to pass through Torres Strait again from east to west.

Cook's Passage

Between May and August 1770, Lieutenant James Cook, in command of HMS *Endeavour*, sailed almost two-thirds the length of the Great Barrier Reef before he 'found' it by running aground on what is now known as Endeavour Reef, about 90 km (56 mi) southeast of Cooktown. Cook's aim had been to make accurate charts of the coast, so he had remained well inshore. He was probably aware of the islands to the east, but not the maze of reefs.

Cook managed to coax the ship north to the mouth of the Endeavour River, the site of Cooktown, where it underwent six weeks of repairs. In the meantime he made his way through the reefs to the north and out to Lizard Island. Here he climbed to the summit, known as Cook's Look, and plotted a course through what is now called Cook's Passage, between the Day and Carter ribbon reefs. A combination of seamanship and a great crew guided the *Endeavour* through the 'labyrinth' and off the Reef.

Definitive proof of Torres Strait was not made known until after Cook's voyage. Although the British knew that a series of reefs off the east coast of the continent existed, they did not realise their extent; Cook's crew and scientists had other priorities – to chart the coastline of this newly discovered 'Great South Land', *Terra Australis Incognita*.

Charting a safe passage

By 1788 the penal colony in Sydney was established, and it was imperative that the British find a shorter and safer passage through the Great Barrier Reef and Torres Strait to the Indian Ocean. A variety of small naval- or government-sponsored surveys were undertaken, but of note is the one carried out by captains Bampton (of the *Shah Hormuzeer*) and Alt (of the *Chesterfield*), who concentrated on Torres Strait in 1793. It was many years before ship's captains were able to feel even relatively safe navigating the Reef, as it was still regarded as one of the world's greatest shipping hazards.

Between 1801 and 1803, the British navigator and cartographer Matthew Flinders surveyed almost the entire Australian coastline on board HMS *Investigator*. He charted some of what he called the 'extensive barrier', tracing a safe passage out of the inner route to the Coral Sea in what is now Flinders Passage. But it was not until the voyages of Matthew Flinders and Nicolas Baudin that the precise extent and configuration of the continent was established, finally bringing to an end centuries of speculation surrounding the mythical and mysterious 'Great South Land' (*Terra Australis Incognita*).

On the HMS *Mermaid* in 1819, and then the HMS *Bathurst* in 1820, Philip Parker King was the first person to chart more of the northern Great Barrier Reef in detail. His chart soundings and coastal and island drawings were still in use in charts in the 1980s. Lieutenant John Lihou, Master of HMS *Zenobia* in 1823, was the first to sail through Torres Strait from west to east.

Between 1842 and 1846, the naturalist and geologist Joseph Jukes and the naturalist John MacGillivray traversed the entire length of the Great Barrier Reef on board HMS *Fly*. They observed the 'luxurant' growth of the coral that was visible at low tide.

Previous spread: An aerial view of Cooktown, on the Endeavour River on Cape York Peninsula.

Above left: *Portrait of William Bampton*, c. 1795?, oil, 57 x 44.5 cm. Bampton kept a journal of his 1793 voyage.

Above centre: HMS *Investigator*, a Royal Navy survey ship.

Above right: *Portrait of Matthew Flinders*, 1870, oil on canvas, 74.0 x 61.5 cm.

Above left: HMS *Mermaid*, which ran aground in 1820, painted by Phillip Parker King.

Above centre: *Portrait of Phillip Parker King*, c. 1816, oil on canvas, 78 x 67 cm, including frame.

Above right: Sir William Beechey, *Portrait of Joseph Beete Jukes as a Young Man*, c. 1840, oil on board, 25.5 x 20.6 cm.

Above far right: HMS *Fly*, an eighteen-gun sloop.

Fast Fact

Raine Island, the most important breeding site for tropical seabirds on the Great Barrier Reef, is now a wildlife sanctuary and closed to the public. Several species of birds nest in a large central depression, caused by the mining of guano in the 1890s.

Safe beacon

The Raine Island beacon, 200 km (124 mi) southeast of Cape York and 600 km (373 mi) north of Cairns, became redundant when the East Channel to the north was found. Visible for more than 20 km (12 mi) and constructed in 1844 by the superb workmanship of convict labour by order of the British Admiralty, it was built of limestone quarried on the island and lime mortar made from burnt clamshells. Originally fitted with timbers from the *Martha Ridgeway*, wrecked on nearby Martha Ridgeway Reef in 1842, its wooden floors, internal stairs and strutted roof with canvas cover are long gone. It became redundant when the Great North East Channel to the north was found.

Although Raine Island is not quite 1 km (½ mi) long, 26,000 green sea turtles have been known to lay their eggs there on a single night. Tiger sharks, which can saw through a turtle shell, lie in wait for them as they return to the sea.

Previous spread: A green sea turtle digs a pit in the sand before laying her eggs, with the Raine Island beacon in the background. The Island is the largest green sea turtle rookery in the world.

Right: A 1786 wood engraving of Aboriginals diving for pearl shells in Torres Strait. Aboriginal men and women as well as Torres Strait Islanders dived for the shells, which were used to make buttons and buckles in Britain and the United States. Pearl-shell diving was a dangerous occupation – divers who went too deep could suffer from 'the bends', or decompression sickness as it is now known; shark attacks and shipwrecks also contributed to the death toll.

Industries in Torres Strait

From the 1860s pearling—primarily for the shells, with pearls a bonus—was a Torres Strait primary industry practised almost as far south as Bathurst Bay on Cape York, but in 1970 the plastics industry nearly resulted in its demise. The industry attracted divers from many countries, especially Japan, to Torres Strait. At the same time there were major beche-de-mer and trochus shell industries.

Lighthouses, originally installed as temporary lights on various islands, were later built as more lasting structures, with each light operated by two families. Lady Elliot Island's first light was a make-shift one, built in 1866; the present day heritage structure, built in 1873, now has an automatic light. Other lighthouses were built on Low Isles (1878), Kent Island (1897) and Russell Island (1929) as well as on many other islands, reefs and shoals; these lights are now run on automatic systems.

In 1879, Queensland—then an established British colony—annexed Torres Strait and Papua New Guinea, and claimed them as part of the colony.

In the 1860s guano mining for agricultural fertiliser began on Lady Elliot, Lady Musgrave, Raine, Northwest, Tryon, Fairfax and Holbourne islands, and continued for about fifty years. Smaller operations were conducted on Upolu, Oyster and Michaelmas reefs. During this period, thousands of tonnes of limestone rock were removed and ground up to reduce the acidity of farm soil. The removal of several metres of guano from Raine Island, creating a crater 1.5 m (5 ft) deep in the middle of the island, has been cited as probably the worst example of human destruction on any of the cays of the Great Barrier Reef.

Fast Fact

After the government imported goats onto Reef islands in the nineteenth century to provide ship-wrecked sailors with a food source, the animals multiplied and stripped islands such as Lady Elliot Island of vegetation. The goats were removed in the late 1970s.

From 1892 to 1900, coconut plantations were established on some Great Barrier Reef islands but, according to the earliest explorers, there were plantations in Torres Strait well before 1700. The Queensland copra (dried coconut meat) trade exported only a few hundred tonnes (tons), so its viability was questionable. The effects of clearing and planting on island vegetation were extensive. Some islands were also cleared for grazing or firewood.

A tourist destination

Basic tourist resorts started to appear in the 1920s on Double, Green and Magnetic islands, which were all serviced from Cairns and Townsville; other resorts in the Whitsunday Islands and on Lady Musgrave Island in the Capricorn and Bunker Group were established in the 1930s.

The Great Barrier Reef Committee (GBRC)—a scientific group formed in 1922 and now known as the Australian Coral Reef Society—noted that the resorts and their patrons were degrading the natural features surrounding the resorts.

By 1940 the old turtle cannery on Heron Island as well as a European settler's cottage on Dunk Island, which had been used as an airstrip and radar base by the Royal Australian Air Force during the Second World War, had both been converted to resorts.

Members of the GBRC conducted expeditions to various parts of the Reef, and also funded the development of the first research facilities, such as Heron Island Research Station, which is now operated by the University of Queensland.

Reports by the marine zoologist Sir Maurice Yonge on his year-long expedition to the Low Isles off Port Douglas in 1928–9 created an enormous amount of scientific interest when he returned to England. The main aim of the expedition was to research the Reef's resource potential, but it yielded far more in scientific studies. The team, which included five Australian Museum scientists, made round-the-clock studies of plants and animals, which now form the basis of many contemporary works. To this day there has been no equivalent 'year on the Great Barrier Reef' study conducted.

Yonge's expedition allowed these scientists to fund their fieldwork on the Great Barrier Reef, especially in the Whitsundays, by taking amateur naturalists and holiday-makers with them. Their quest was to hunt specimens of creatures they could collect and preserve. Many areas, including Low Isles, were swept clean by collectors. These visitors often decimated the reef tops exposed at low tide and dredged lagoon floors for molluscs, in the process destroying large areas of beautiful but fragile coral colonies.

Opposite: Photographs of Heron Island, taken by Frank Hurley (1885-1962) between 1910 and 1962, but probably in the 1940s.

Photographs clockwise from top left:

Under torchlight provided by a group of enthusiastic observers, a sea turtle lays her eggs.

A spearfisher displays her modest catch.

Riding a giant turtle, definitely not an approved activity for today's tourists.

A view of the tourist resort at Heron Island, a typical low-lying coral cay.

A day's haul. (Although Hurley's own handwritten note attributes the image to Heron Island, it is almost certainly Thursday Island.)

It was in 1947, when a Catalina flying boat started flying direct from Brisbane to Heron Island lagoon, that the Great Barrier Reef tourism industry became firmly established. Another innovation was the introduction of the underwater observatory at the end of the jetty at Green Island in the 1950s; about fifteen years later, another was built at Hook Island. As the coral colonies died off, these observatories kept their underwater displays looking their best by collecting live corals from nearby habitats.

By the late 1960s, with about a million people visiting some part of the Reef each year, the impact of tourism had become obvious. The combination of sewage outfalls, the over-collection of reef-top species, over-fishing near the resort reefs, and the construction of jetties, marinas, channels and airstrips resulted in massive changes—cays lost significant parts of their leeward ends; seagrass beds, enriched by sewage, formed on reef tops; and reef sections died off due to poorer water quality as a result of earthworks and other activities. Human hair, wire, string and rope became entangled in the legs of birds. In addition, turtles, fish and other animals died after ingesting plastics and other materials.

In 1950 William Dakin published the first popular scientific view of the Reef; this was followed by many populist books as well as scientific papers and significant books. All carried the same message—the Reef had to be conserved properly.

Previous spread and opposite: Green Island and its pier, which are accessible from Cairns, the nearest jump-off point.

Environmental catastrophes

Extensive destruction of island habitats and the integrity of the islands themselves resulted from not only the guano miners and goats but also the beche-de-mer fishermen—who cut down the timber so they could preserve their product by smoking it—and then tourism. Other destructive activities included introducing exotic species, blasting channels through reefs, clearing vegetation, quarrying, grazing and even military target practice.

Introduced ants and other animal species have also had a catastrophic effect on native species. Even today there are proposals for blasting and dredging harbours on Great Barrier Reef islands. The continuing extensive dredging associated with coastal ports has a devastating effect on marine life.

Right: Lizard Island, the larger island in the background, is now a national park that also includes an Australian Museum research station and a tourist resort.

In the mid-1960s, scientists and the public had begun to agitate for better protection of the Reef's islands and reefs, and one of the biggest conservation efforts in Australia's history—the 'Save the Great Barrier Reef' campaign—went into full swing. In 1974, after the whole Province was found to be under oil exploration leases and it was proposed to dredge thousands of tonnes of coral from Ellison Reef near Innisfail, a Royal Commission into Oil Drilling on the Great Barrier Reef was called. Research stations on various islands—such as Low Isles and One Tree and Lizard islands (Australian Museum), Heron Island (University of Queensland) and Orpheus Island (James Cook University)— were also established or expanded.

The Australian Institute of Marine Science was established in 1972, and it immediately began to research many aspects of the Reef, focusing on fish, coral taxonomy—that is, identifying and naming coral species—and physiology, mangroves and water quality, complementing and developing the work undertaken by the Commonwealth Scientific and Industrial Research Organisation and the universities and museums that were already active. The institute also studied marine biodiversity; the impact of, and adaptation to, climate change; water quality; and ecosystem health.

Fisheries, offshore oil and gas, mining, Reef tourism and aquaculture industries have all benefited from the institute's research, which is geared towards the protection and sustainable development of marine resources. These benefits will help ensure protection of Australia's marine biodiversity and new areas of the economy into the future.

Literary campaigns

The Coral Battleground (1977), by the Australian poet and writer Judith Wright, is a gripping account of the struggle to save the reef and establish the Great Barrier Reef Marine Park. Other publications worth reading are Patricia Clare's *The Struggle for the Great Barrier Reef* (1971) and Isobel Bennett's *The Great Barrier Reef* (1971). In 1994 Wright said: 'If we have in fact lost the "coral battle" we have also lost the world itself, since the Reef is a microcosm of the fading natural world.'

Above: The Heron Island Research Station, which is run and operated by the University of Queensland. This station is one of many research stations set up after a Royal Commission into Oil Drilling on the Great Barrier Reef was called.

World Heritage Area & Region Boundary

Great Barrier Reef Marine Park

Great Barrier Reef Province
(As defined by W.G.H. Maxwell)

Papua New Guinea

Cape Flattery
Cooktown

Cairns

Innisfail
Mission Beach

Townsville

Airlie Beach

Mackay

Gladstone

Bundaberg

Queensland

Above: The boundaries of The Great Barrier Reef. For more information, see page 5.

Great Barrier Reef Marine Park Authority

It was not until 1975 that the Great Barrier Reef Marine Park Authority (GBRMPA) was established to ensure the long-term sustainable use of the Reef while allowing reasonable use of its resources. To achieve this, the authority implemented a system of Zoning Plans, which change every five years or so.

In 1981 the Great Barrier Reef World Heritage Area—including not only the GBRMP but also all the islands and coastal areas that had been excluded from the marine park—was placed on the International Union for Conservation of Nature (IUCN) Register. It then became the Australian government's responsibility to ensure the Reef was properly protected and also to prevent any oil drilling or mining to occur within it.

Due to the complexities of managing the resources of Torres Strait and also to respect the Traditional Owners' rights, in 1978 the Australian and Papuan New Guinean governments formed a maritime border in Torres Strait. Since then a co-operative management plan has been in use.

In May 2007 the Australian World Heritage property of the Great Barrier Reef was transferred onto the National Heritage List for its World Heritage value. There are also five Commonwealth Heritage places within the Great Barrier Reef Region as well as places of historical significance, including lighthouses and shipwrecks, which are managed to protect heritage values.

The future of the Great Barrier Reef

Reefs all over the world are recognised as the thermometers of global health. They face climate change, diminishing water quality, and destruction of marine and nearby land habitats for logging, agriculture, mining and urbanisation. They also face ocean acidification, over-fishing, illegal fishing and poaching. All these factors affect the ability of reef systems to survive and adapt. In some parts of the world reefs are in dire straits, while others are either surviving or, like the GBR, in decline. This is despite the increased efforts of environmental authorities in all aspects affecting the Reef's health. The Great Barrier Reef is at a crossroad and the actions of people and organisations over the next few years will help determine its future. Climate change, and the Reef's resilience to this, will be a huge factor in its future survival.

It is very clear that humans are having an effect on greenhouse gases. By taking core samples from lake floors, coral, ice and sediments, scientists have found dust, pollen and ashes indicating the climates of times past. We know that four glaciations have occurred in the last 400,000 years. During each glaciation, the Great Barrier Reef was exposed as dry limestone hills for up to 30,000 years at a time. This means that, given the right circumstances, coral reefs are very resilient systems. However, the current stresses represent a challenge they have never faced before.

We do not know of any reef system that is not showing signs of stress, which can be seen as chronic bleaching events (primarily as a result of increases in water temperature); reduction in species diversity, sometimes with local extinctions; changes in habitat structure; and diseases occurring in the corals. There are also areas where sponges and algae are growing over what were until recently healthy colonies of coral; the coral has lost its ability to fight off these organisms. When coral colonies are healthy, this is not an issue.

Opposite: The Queensland Nickel Refinery at Yabulu, which is about 25 km (15 mi) north of Townsville.

Fast Fact

Research shows that the loss of corals results in the loss of many other species reliant on them for food and shelter, or for the food and shelter of their prey.

There have been five major extinction events and twenty minor ones in the past 3.5 billion years (see page 137). It seems we are headed for another major global extinction event.

The last glaciation event, which occurred about 18,000 years ago, lowered the sea level by 130 m (426 ft). During this period, the coral reef plants and animals would have migrated out onto the edge of the continental shelf and ocean outliers, such as the reefs on the Coral Sea Rise. They have also survived other massive changes in global climate due to such geological events as volcanic eruptions and tectonic plate uplifts.

Decreasing water quality

There are many ways to determine if coral reefs are stressed, compared to much healthier systems of only a few decades ago. Coastal development on the Great Barrier Reef began in the 1860s (see page 206). The resulting land clearing and coastal runoff from overgrazed and unprotected lands has seen the destruction of the fringing reefs along the mainland coast, especially south of Cooktown. Some near-shore reefs, seagrass beds and sea-floor communities are also deteriorating as they become smothered by silt.

Coral bleaching

Although the bleaching of corals has been observed for decades, in the last ten years much greater areas have been affected. Massive bleaching events, which can be seen from the air at 7000 m (23,000 ft) or more above sea level, indicate that the coral is in stress from chemicals, temperature, salinity and over-exposure to bright sunlight.

The bleaching usually occurs in hotter water and also during long periods of calm, hot days, allowing the zooxanthellae to produce more oxygen than normal. They become toxic to the coral, and the polyps eject them from their tissues. This makes the polyps fade from their usual dark pastel browns, blues, greens and yellows through beautiful soft pastel colours until they become totally transparent, and you can see the white calcium carbonate skeleton underneath the coral animal. If you look underwater, the bleaching creates an eerie effect.

Some species of coral are more tolerant of the causes of bleaching and will remain 'normally

coloured'—that is, full of their zooxanthellae—but other colonies turn white. There are several species of zooxanthellae, so some may allow some corals to survive the stress period. If the temperature change is fast and the coral colony is able to retain some of its zooxanthellae, then it may recover. Should the stressors last for longer periods, the corals may die off completely.

Current research indicates that the long-term future of the Great Barrier Reef's ability to with-stand chronic bleaching events, which are occurring more frequently and for longer periods, is severely compromised. The Intergovernmental Panel on Climate Change (IPCC) predicts a 2°C (35.6°F) rise in global seawater temperatures in the next twenty years., which would have a serious effect on the Great Barrier Reef.

Above: Coral becomes bleached when its resident colourful algae, called zooxanthellae, become toxic to the coral. They then expell the algae, which leave behind colourless colonies like this one.

Right: The survival of many species of mollusc, such as the cone shell, which inhabits mud and sand flats on the Great Barrier Reef, is threatened by ocean acidification.

Ocean acidification

As global carbon dioxide levels increase, more of it dissolves into the ocean, making it more acidic. There are many data sets explaining how this occurs in a seawater that is almost saturated with calcium carbonate and thus should be able to buffer itself and remain alkaline, but the chemical reactions that occur do not show this. Even small rises of carbon dioxide in the atmosphere cause more acidic waters.

There are many plants and animals—including coralline algae, planktonic and bottom-dwelling crustaceans, shells and corals—that rely on the calcium carbonate from seawater to grow their skeletons. If one of these is removed from the complex food webs in which they play important roles, then it is easy to predict bizarre collapses of the webs. The krill in Antarctic waters will also be compromised—what will be the effect on the penguins and whales that rely on them?

Sea level changes

Slow changes in rising sea levels will allow corals to keep up their growth, but falling levels will result in the colonies being grazed and/or eroded off, usually to the average low tide level. When the channel was blasted out at Heron Island, there were several massive effects: first, about 20 m (22 yd) of the beaches around the island were eroded away, then the 'tail' of sand on the western end of the cay disappeared out the channel and, finally, the water level in the western lagoon dropped due to the extra drainage. It took some years, but the whole coral and algal reef top on the western end of the Reef dropped about 10 cm (4 in).

The coral cays and many sand banks on the mainland islands were formed from the coral growth during the three periods of high sea level over the last 5000 years. The reef growth created a supply of material that was affected by physical or biological erosion, and the resultant sands and rubble were dumped onto the reef tops as cays or rubble/shingle banks. In some cases it filled in lagoons but in others it simply washed off the back of each reef.

Fast Fact

Coral skeletal material will be weakened by more acidic waters, thus creating 'weaker' reef growths, which could cause reefs to become eroding rather than growth features.

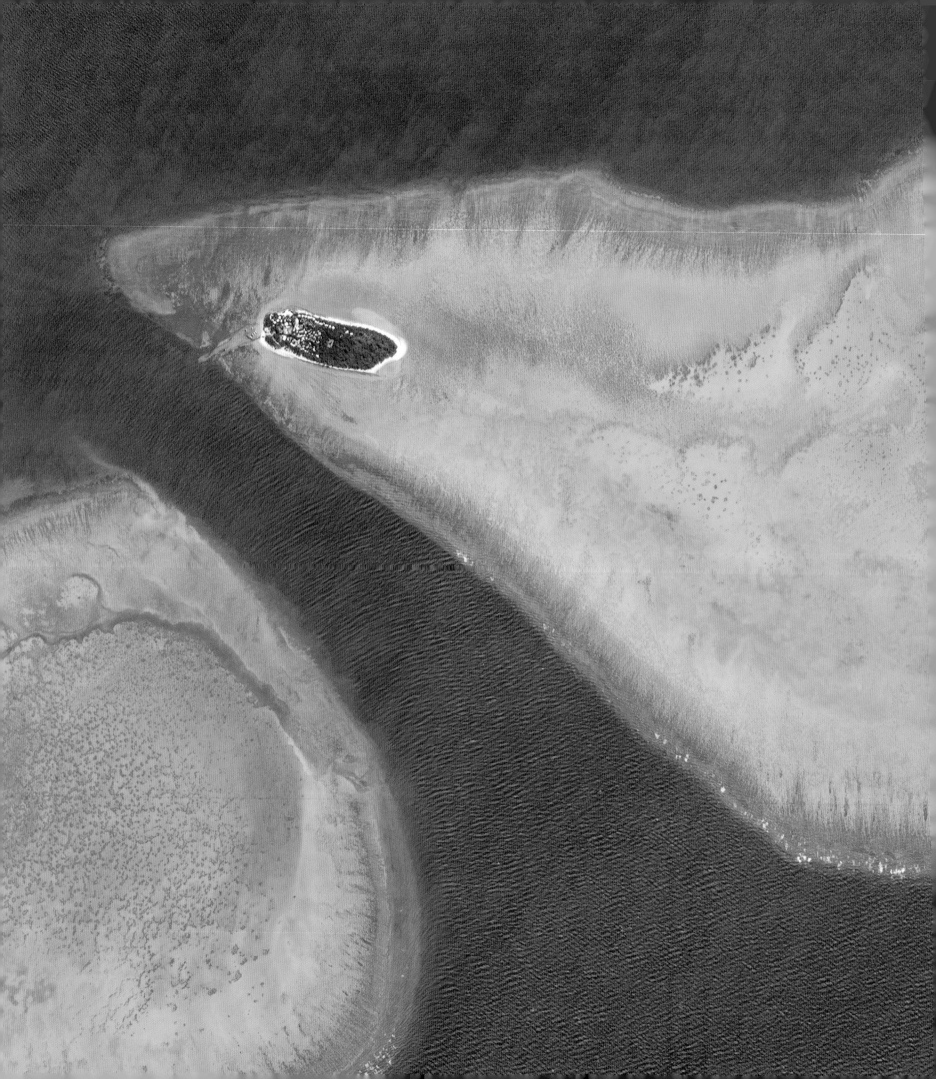

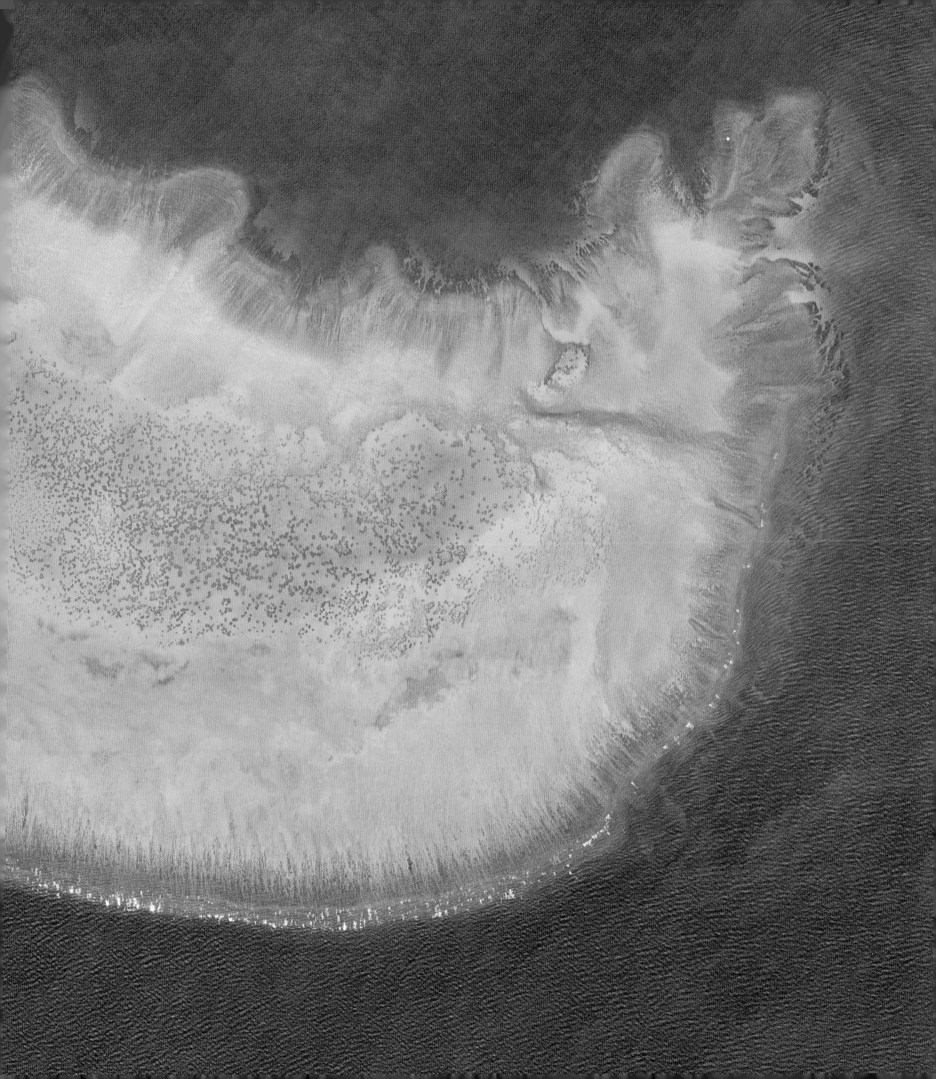

Previous spread: Heron Island Channel. The narrow channel leading from the marina to the ocean was blasted and dredged decades ago, before the island became a national park. Since then the Australian government has implemented conservation measures, such as limiting the number of tourists as well as removing or recycling rubbish, rather than incinerating it.

Opposite: This staghorn coral has been eaten by the crown-of-thorns sea star in the foreground. Note the healthy brown coral to the right.

Weather changes

As climate change occurs over hundreds or thousands of years, and weather is a daily manifestation of those changes, we must expect constantly changing weather patterns. Our present accurate records only go back about 100 years, but there is a lot of other data that gives us good information on climate. Twenty thousand years ago, when the Great Barrier Reef was high and dry, and the sea level was 130 m (426 ft) below its present level, Australia was a much more arid continent.

It is predicted that we will experience more severe weather patterns, such as storms, 'microbursts', or mini-tornados, the cyclones of the southern hemisphere and the typhoons, hurricanes and tornados of the northern hemisphere.

More severe weather can result in higher river outflows, affecting the quality of coastal water and resulting in the re-suspension of bottom sediments in shallower waters. This in turn affects the sea-floor communities over which these resulting water masses move. Should wave frequency and size increase on the Great Barrier Reef, this would also have dramatic effects.

Coral diseases

In stressed colonies, pathogenic bacteria are the greatest cause of coral diseases. Of the thirty coral diseases that occur worldwide, black-band, brown-band, white syndrome, skeletal eroding band, black necrosing band, pink spot and coral tumours occur on the Reef. To date the research from the Australian Institute of Marine Science and James Cook University indicates that the diseases themselves are not a threat to the Reef but we do not know whether this will continue to be the case.

Weakened corals are also vulnerable to predators and other organisms. For example, some molluscs, and sponges and, in some cases, algae will quickly colonise dead skeletal areas, minimising the chances of new polyp larvae colonising the area.

How corals can adapt

Research shows that corals can adapt to some degree, and they may be able to evolve in order to adapt to the new conditions resulting from climate change, but we still do not know for sure.

What can we do?

Most governments in countries with coral reefs are under pressure to better protect and manage their remaining reef systems and, ideally, to restore them as much as possible. This is especially evident when they understand that an unhealthy reef can lead to a decline in tourism revenues and poorer coastal communities—both human and natural. And once the protective reef is destroyed, the forces of the sea can destroy the coast.

The Great Barrier Reef, one of the great natural wonders of the world, is accepted as a global 'icon'. The Queensland tourism industry generates about $6 billion annually from the Reef alone. When compared with the returns from primary industries of $14.69 billion—which includes fisheries, mining of fuel minerals, forestry products, non-metallic minerals and metallic minerals—it is possible to see the economic importance of the Great Barrier Reef as a resource for fisheries and especially tourism, hence the need for sustainable practices to be put in place as soon as possible.

As each community begins to develop reef research, education and management systems, we will see the establishment of more marine parks and the sharing of knowledge by all means possible. But even with an active global policy of restricting increases in greenhouse gases and reducing levels of carbon dioxide, we are still likely to see reefs subjected to higher temperatures and lower carbonate levels than they have experienced for millions of years. Bleaching events will continue to increase, reef structures will decline and then, as carbon dioxide levels begin to decrease again, we can expect an increasing abundance in the success of carbonate-reliant plants and corals and also of the plants and animals that rely on them.

Opposite: If the Great Barrier Reef is to survive in the long term, we need to do our utmost to conserve and protect this natural wonder.

Given the strong management of the Great Barrier Reef, it is likely that the ecosystem will survive better under the pressure of accumulating risks than most reef systems around the world. However, even with the recent management initiatives to improve resilience, the overall outlook for the Great Barrier Reef is poor, and catastrophic damage to the ecosystem may not be averted. Ultimately, if changes in the world's climate become too severe, no management actions will be able to climate-proof the Great Barrier Reef ecosystem.

Further building the resilience of the Great Barrier Reef by improving water quality, reducing the loss of coastal habitats and increasing knowledge about fishing and its effects, will give it the best chance of adapting to, and recovering from, the serious threats ahead, especially from climate change.

GBRMPA, 2009

APPENDIX

GLOSSARY

abyssal depths from 4000 to 6000 m (13,123 to 19,685 ft) below sea level

anemones or sea anemones most species are column-shaped polyps with an adhesive foot at the base and tentacles at the 'mouth' end

beche-de-mer sea cucumber, a delicacy (fresh or dried) in Eastern and Southeast Asian cuisines

bi-valves molluscs whose bodies are enclosed by two shells—for example, oysters and clams

bioluminescence the production of light by a living organism

biomass biological material from living or decomposing organisms

bommies an outcrop of rock and coral

bryozoans lace coral

ciguatera a form of food poisoning caused by eating reef fish contaminated with toxins produced by micro-organisms called dinoflagelletes

cilia tiny hair-like projections on the surfaces of some organisms

cnidarian animals an enormous group of animals that possess specially modified cells called nematocysts, or stinging cells. This group includes sea jellies, anemones, sea whips, zooanthids, corallimorparians, stinging hydroids, hard corals and soft corals

commensal an organism that benefits from living with another organism without harming or benefiting it

coral bommie see Bommie

coral coring drilling and removing a core sample from coral for research purposes

coralline resembling coral

crystalline resembling crystal

culvert drain

cuspate ribbon reefs ribbon reefs that form a triangular elongated growth

detrital feeders or detrivores organisms that feed off decomposing plants and animals

diatomaceous earths the fossilised remains of a type of hard shelled algae called diatoms; they are used for, among other things, filters, cat litter and pest repellents in gardens

families, genera and species all plants and animals are classified according to the family they belong to; they are then subdivided into genera (plural for 'genus') and again into species—for example, the humpback whale (*Megaptera novaeangliae*) is a member of the Balaenopteridae family (that is, baleen whales, which have baleen plates for filtering food from water, rather than teeth), and it also belongs to the genus *Megaptera*, and to the species *Megaptera novaeangliae*

flotsam is floating wreckage from a ship or its cargo

Foraminiferans are the most common marine plankton species

foram sand sand made up of the tiny shells of single-celled organisms called foraminfera

free-living organism one that is not directly dependent on another

organism for survival—for example, sharks swim freely and depend only on other organisms for food

gamete a cell that fuses with another cell during fertilisation; in organisms that reproduce sexually, one gamete may be the ovum or egg and the other the sperm

gastropods are a class of molluscs, including sea snails, whelks, abalone, conches and periwinkles

glaciation ice age characterised by lower temperatures and the advance of glaciers

guano the urine and faeces of birds, cave-dwelling bats and seals that is used as a garden fertiliser

heathlands areas of low-growing shrubs where the soil is too poor to support the growth of trees

humic substances major organic constituents, usually in soils

hydrographer someone who charts a body of water by measuring its depths, tides and currents, usually to establish a safe passage for shipping

hydroids cnidarian feather-like animals with stinging capsules

interstitial spaces the gaps between matter, such as the gaps between grains of sand

invertebrate animal species without a backbone

jetsam is a part of a ship, or its associated equipment or cargo that is deliberately cast overboard to lighten the load if the ship finds itself in distress

K-T Extinction the period when dinosaurs became extinct about 65 million years ago—'K' stands for the Cretaceous Period and 'T' for the Tertiary Period

leeward is the direction downwind from the point of reference

macroalgae seaweeds

microbes single-celled organisms, including viruses and bacteria, that cannot be seen without a microscope

nematocysts stinging capsules in cnidarian animals, such as jellyfish

ooze fine mud on the sea floor that is full of decaying life forms

ooze dwellers those organisms that live off the *ooze* on the sea floor

operculum little lid or 'trapdoor' used by such gastropods as sea snails to close the opening of its shell

plankton or planktonic organisms any (usually microscopic) animals, plants, algae or bacteria that drift in the ocean

proboscis usually refers to the nose or snout in vertebrate animals, or to a long protruding part on an invertebrate

rain shadow a dry area on the lee side of a mountain range

runoff excess water from rain flows off the land into rivers and, ultimately, into the sea

sedges a family of flowering plants that look like grasses or rushes

sedimentation the build-up of silt and sediment against a barrier

semi-terrestrial organisms, such as sand crabs, that do not live entirely on land

shoals sandbanks or sand bars

strandline the high water mark on a beach where waves deposit flotsam and jetsam

substrate mud, rocks or sand at the bottom of a marine environment

synaptid referring to tentacles at the end of a sea cucumber which it cannot retract into the body cavity

terrestrial living on land, rather than in the sea

thalli vegetative tissue of some organisms such as algae, fungus and lichens—for example, seaweed may look as if it has branches or stems and leaves but marine biologists class the whole organism as a thallus

turf algae algae that grow in turf-like structures

vertebrate animal species that have a backbone or spinal column

water column any vertical body of water, from the sea floor to the surface

watershed a mountain range, ridge or peak that separates water catchment areas

zooplankton small floating aquatic animals

zooxanxthellae microscopic algae that live in the tissues of coral polyps

BIBLIOGRAPHY

Gerald R. Allen and Roger C. Steene, *Indo-Pacific Coral Reef Guide: Tropical Reef Research*, University of California, Berkeley, 1994.

Gerald R. Allen, Roger Swainston and Jill Ruse, *Marine Fishes of Tropical Australia and South-East Asia*, Western Australia Museum, Perth, 1997.

Robert G.V. Baker, Robert J. Haworth and G. Peter Flood, 'An Oscillating Holocene Sea-level? Revisiting Rottnest Island, Western Australia and the Fairbridge Eustatic Hypothesis', *Journal of Coastal Research*, vol. 42, 2004, pp. 3–14.

Isobel Bennett, *Australia's Great Barrier Reef*, Collins/Australian Museum, Sydney, 1987.

Isobel Bennett, *A Coral Reef Handbook*, Australian Coral Reef Society, Brisbane, 1978.

Isobel Bennett, *The Fringe of the Sea*, Rigby, Adelaide, 1966.

Isobel Bennett, *The Great Barrier Reef*, Lansdowne Press, Sydney, 1971.

Isobel Bennett, *On the Seashore*, Rigby, Adelaide, 1969.

William Bligh, Logbook of HMS *Providence*: http://www.fatefulvoyage.com/providenceBligh/920908.html

James Bowen and Margarita Bowen, *The Great Barrier Reef: History, Science, Heritage*, Cambridge University Press, Melbourne, 2002.

Margarita Bowen, quoted in WiseNet, Journal 34. Go to: www.wisenet-australia.org, March 1994, pp. 13–14.

John Brodie and Katharina Fabricius in Pat Hutchings, Mike Kingsford and Ove Hoegh-Guldberg (eds), *The Great Barrier Reef: Biology, Environment and Management*, CSIRO Publishing, Melbourne, 2008.

Patricia Clare, *The Struggle for the Great Barrier Reef*, Collins, London, 1971.

Harold G. Cogger, *Reptiles and Amphibians of Australia*, 6th edn, Reed New Holland, Sydney, 2000.

Leonard Cronin, *Cronin's Key Guide: Australian Mammals*, Allen & Unwin, Sydney, 2008.

Leonard Cronin, *Key Guide: Australian Reptiles and Amphibians*, Envirobook, Sydney, 2001.

W.J. Dakin, *The Great Barrier Reef*, National Publicity Association, Melbourne, 1950.

W.J. Dakin, *The Great Barrier Reef and Some Mention of Other Australian Coral Reefs*, National Publicity Association, Melbourne, 1950.

Ben Daley and Peter Griggs, 'Mining the Reefs and Cays: Coral, Guano and Rock Phosphate Extraction in the Great Barrier Reef, 1844–1940', *Environment and History*, vol. 12, no. 4, 2006, pp. 395–433.

Alexander Dalrymple, *Historical Collection of the Several Voyages and Discoveries in the South Pacific Ocean in 1770–1771*, 1770–71 (full text available online).

G. Diaz-Pulido in Pat Hutchings, Mike Kingsford and Ove Hoegh-Guldberg (eds), *The Great Barrier Reef: Biology, Environment and Management*, CSIRO Publishing, Melbourne, 2008, pp. 146–56.

Graham J. Edgar, *Australian Marine Habitats in Temperate Waters*, New Holland, Sydney, 2001.

Graham J. Edgar, *Australian Marine Life: The Plants and Animals of Temperate Waters*, Reed Books, Melbourne, 2007.

Josephine Flood, *The Original Australians: Story of the Aboriginal People*, Allen & Unwin, Sydney, 2006.

Great Barrier Reef Marine Park Authority, *GBR Outlook Report 2009 GBRMPA*, 2009.

Great Barrier Reef Marine Park Authority, *Map of the GBR Marine Park Region*, 1975.

Great Barrier Reef Marine Park Authority, *Map of the GBR World Heritage Area*, 1981.

Ernie Grant, *Guide to Fishes*, 11th edn, E. M. Grant, Redcliffe North, Queensland, 2008.

Brett Hilder, *The Voyage of Torres*, University of Queensland Press, Brisbane, 1980.

Ove Hoegh-Guldberg, 'Epilogue', in Pat Hutchings, Mike Kingsford and Ove Hoegh-Guldberg (eds), *The Great Barrier Reef: Biology, Environment and Management*, CSIRO Publishing, Melbourne, 2008, pp. 369–70.

John Hooper in Pat Hutchings, Mike Kingsford and Ove Hoegh-Guldberg (eds), *The Great Barrier Reef: Biology, Environment and Management*, CSIRO Publishing, Melbourne, 2008.

D. Hopley, *Geomorphology of the Great Barrier Reef: Quarternary Development of Coral Reefs*, John Wiley Interscience, New York, 1982.

D. Hopley, S.G. Smithers and K.E. Parnell, *The Geomorphology of the Great Barrier Reef: Development, Diversity and Change*, Cambridge University Press, Cambridge, 2007.

Pat Hutchings, Mike Kingsford and Ove Hoegh-Guldberg (eds), *The Great Barrier Reef: Biology, Environment and Management*, CSIRO Publishing, Melbourne, 2008.

David Johnson, *The Geology of Australia*, Cambridge University Press, Cambridge, 2004.

P.R. Last and J.D. Stevens, *Sharks and Rays of Australia*, CSIRO Publishing, Melbourne, 1994.

Sam Leonardi, personal communication with author, 1999.

C.J. Limpus, *A Biological Review of Australian Marine Turtles: 2* Chelonia mydas *(Linnaeus)*, Queensland Environmental Protection Agency, 2008.

K.J. Lohmann, 'Magnetic orientation by hatchling loggerhead sea turtles (*Caretta caretta*)', *Journal of Experimental Biology*, no. 155, 1991, pp. 37–49.

W.G.H. Maxwell, *Atlas of the Great Barrier Reef*, Elsevier Publishing, Amsterdam, 1968.

K.G. McIntyre, *The Secret Discovery of Australia: Portuguese Ventures 200 Years Before Cook*, Souvenir Press, Menindie, 1977.

K.G. McIntyre, *The Secret Discovery of Australia: Portuguese Ventures 250 Years Before Captain Cook*, Pan Books, Sydney, 1982.

P. Menkhorst and Frank Knight, *A Field Guide to the Mammals of* Australia, Oxford University Press, Melbourne, 2010.

Michael Morcombe, *Field Guide to Australian Birds*, Steve Parish Publishing, Briabane, 2004.

Graham Pizzey (author) and Frank Knight (illustrator), *The Field Guide to the Birds of Australia*, HarperCollins, Sydney, 2007.

Queensland government, Department of Primary Industries website, Got to: www.dpi. qld.gov.au/16_9795.htm

Queensland Annual Mineral Summary, 2009-10, Go to: www.mines.industry.qld. gov.au/assets/minerals-pdf/mineral-table-09-10.pdf

John E. Randall, Gerald R. Allen and Roger C. Steene, *Fishes of the Great Barrier Reef and Coral Sea*, University of Hawaii Press, Honolulu, 1996.

D. Raup and J. Sepkoski Jr, 'Mass extinctions in the marine fossil record', *Science*, vol. 215, no. 539, 1982, pp. 1501–3.

Henry Reynolds, *Aboriginal Sovereignty: Reflections on Race, State and Nation*, Allen & Unwin, Sydney, 1996.

Henry Reynolds (ed.), *Aborigines and Settlers: The Australian Experience, 1788–1939*, Cassell Australia, Melbourne, 1972.

Henry Reynolds, *Dispossession: Black Australia and White Invaders*, Allen & Unwin, Sydney, 1989.

Henry Reynolds, *Fate of a Free People*, Penguin, Melbourne, 2004.

Henry Reynolds, *Frontier: Aborigines, Settlers and Land*, Allen & Unwin, Sydney, 1996.

Henry Reynolds, *An Indelible Stain: The Question of Genocide in Australia's History*, Viking, Melbourne, 2001.

Henry Reynolds, *The Law of the Land*, Penguin, Melbourne, 2003.

Henry Reynolds, *The Other Side of the Frontier: Aboriginal Resistance to the European Invasion of Australia*, Penguin, Melbourne, 1982.

Henry Reynolds, *Why Weren't We Told? A Personal Search for the Truth About Our History*, Penguin, Melbourne, 2000.

William Saville-Kent, *The Great Barrier Reef of Australia: Its Products and Potentialities*, W.H. Allen, London, 1893.

Ken Simpson and Nicholas Day, *Field Guide to the Birds of Australia, 8th edn*, Viking (Penguin Books), Melbourne, Victoria, 2010.

Peter Slater, Pat Slater and Raoul Slater, *The Slater Field Guide to Australian Birds*, 2nd edn, New Holland, Sydney, 2009.

Struan K. Sutherland, *Venomous Creatures of Australia: A Field Guide with Notes on First Aid*, Oxford University Press, Melbourne, 2006.

P. Trickett, *Beyond Capricorn: How Portuguese Adventurers Secretly Discovered and Mapped Australia and New Zealand 250 Years Before Captain Cook,* East Street Publications, Adelaide, 2007.

Barbara Triggs, *Tracks, Scats and Other Traces: A Field Guide to Australian Mammals*, 3rd edn, Oxford University Press, Melbourne, 1996.

Steve Van Dyck and Ronald Strahan (eds), *The Mammals of Australia*, 3rd edn, Reed New Holland, Melbourne, 2008.

J.E.N. Veron, personal communication with the author, 2012.

J.E.N. Veron, *A Reef in Time: The Great Barrier Reef from Beginning to End*, Harvard University Press, Cambridge, MA, 2009.

J.E.N. Veron, *Corals of Australia and the Indo-Pacific*, Australian Institute of Marine Science, Sydney, 1986.

J.E.N. Vernon, *Corals in Space and Time: The Biogeography and Evolution of the Scleractinia*, University of New South Wales Press, Sydney, 1995.

J.E.N. Vernon, *Corals of the World*, Vols 1–3, Australian Institute of Marine Science, Sydney, 2000. Keith Windschuttle, *The Fabrication of Aboriginal History, Volume One: Van Diemen's Land 1803–1847*, Macleay Press, Sydney, 2002.

Keith Windschuttle, *The Fabrication of Aboriginal History, Volume Three: The Stolen Generations 1881–2008*, Macleay Press, Sydney, 2009.

Judith Wright, *The Coral Battleground*, HarperCollins, Sydney, 1996.

Judith Wright, quoted in WiseNet, Journal 34. Go to: www.wisenet-australia.org/profiles/JudithWright.htm.

C.M. Yonge, *A Year on the Great Barrier Reef: The Story of Corals and of the Greatest of Their Creations*, Putnam, London, 1930.

L.D. Zell, *Great Barrier Reef Foundation – Establishment Consultant's Report*, unpublished, 1996.

USEFUL INFORMATION

General information

Great Barrier Reef Marine Park Authority (GBRMPA), Go to: www.gbrmpa.gov.au

Queensland Marine Parks,
Go to: www.derm.qld.gov.au

Camping

For permits and information,
Go to: www.derm.qld.gov.au

For information on Torres Strait Islands camping, contact The Torres Strait Regional Authority, Go to:
http://www.tsra.gov.au/

Fishing

To report suspected emergency and animal diseases, phone the Emergency Animal Diseases Watch Hotline on 1800 675 888.

To report suspected exotic plant pests, phone the Exotic Plant Pest Hotline on 1800 084 881.

To report out-of-place shark equipment or trapped marine animals, phone the Shark Hotline on 1800 806 891.

To report illegal fishing activities, phone the Fishwatch Hotline on 1800 017 116.

To report your catch of tagged fish, phone the Tagged Fish Hotline on 1800 077 001.

PICTURE CREDITS

INDEX

ACKNOWLEDGEMENTS

There have been an enormous number of people who have helped me on my journey to write this book. I especially want to thank Richard Pearson for his support and help with the text in general. Peter Gesner and Jenny Freeman who helped me to ensure my writings on the history of the Reef were correct, and Neville Zell for his overall comments and support. If there are any mistakes in this book, they are mine through misinterpretation.

I have also received support from Peter and Beryl Beinssen, Barbara Pearson, Jim and Margie Zell, Charlie Veron, Leon Zann, Terry Done, John Barnett, charter boat operators, resorts, research stations and all the staff at the University of New England, James Cook University, Australian Institute of Marine Science, Great Barrier Reef Marine Park Authority and other organisations that have helped in the development of my knowledge throughout the forty years I have worked on the Great Barrier Reef. It was this experience that has enabled me to write this book.

I also wish to thank the staff at Murdoch Books for their general good humour and professionalism, particularly the publisher, Paul Mitchell. I would particularly like to acknowledge their careful selection and captioning of the images.

And finally, I would like to acknowledge my hero, Isobel Bennett, who sadly passed away recently. Her inspirational actions helped me achieve so much more Great Barrier Reef success than I would have without her.

DEDICATION

This book is dedicated to the late Isobel Bennett, who was Australia's leading authority on the intertidal organisms found on our coasts. She also wrote nine books, kept William Dakin's Australian Seashores book alive long after his death (ultimately as first author) and taught hundreds of students the excitement of our seas and reefs. She was awarded an MSc (the first honorary one from the University of Sydney), a DSc (Honours, University of New South Wales) and an AO for her contributions to marine science. One of the first women to join an expedition with Australian Antarctic Research Expeditions (ANARE)—to Macquarie Island—Bennett also had several species of animals and orchids named after her. She made numerous visits to the Great Barrier Reef from as early as 1954 onwards, and wrote the first definitive book on the Great Barrier Reef. She was a stunning inspiration to many.

Published in 2012 by Murdoch Books Pty Limited

Murdoch Books Australia
Pier 8/9
23 Hickson Road
Millers Point NSW 2000
Phone: +61 (0) 2 8220 2000
Fax: +61 (0) 2 8220 2558
www.murdochbooks.com.au
info@murdochbooks.com.au

Murdoch Books UK Limited
Erico House, 6th Floor
93-99 Upper Richmond Road
Putney, London SW15 2TG
Phone: +44 (0) 20 8785 5995
Fax: +44 (0) 20 8785 5985
www.murdochbooks.co.uk
info@murdochbooks.co.uk

For Corporate Orders & Custom Publishing contact Noel Hammond,
National Business Development Manager, Murdoch Books Australia

Chief Executive Officer: Matt Handbury
Publishing Director: Chris Rennie
Designer: Russell Whittle
Editor: Sarah Baker
Project Editor: Kit Carstairs
Picture Researcher: Will Jones
Researchers: Rachel Butler (BBC) and Maggie Gowan (BBC)
Illustrator: Andrew McWhae
Production: Mike Crowton

The BBC/Digital Dimensions TV Series, *Great Barrier Reef*, inspired the idea for
this book. Murdoch Books would like to acknowledge the following from BBC Worldwide:
Neil Nightingale (Global Creative Director)
Jacob de Boer (Global Commercial Director)
Heather McIlfatrick (Head of Commercial, Australia)
Sharon Wilson (Head of Marketing, Australia)

Extracts from the Great Barrier Reef 2009 Outlook Report ©GBRMPA:
Reproduced with the permission of the Great Barrier Reef Marine Park Authority.

A cataloguing-in-publication entry is available from the catalogue
of the National Library of Australia at www.nla.gov.au

A catalogue record for this book is available from the British Library.

Printed by Hang Tai, China.